T0304786

Communication

Roger Cartwright

LEADING

08.08

- ■ *The* fast track route to mastering all aspects of successful communication

- ■ Covers the key areas of communication, from knowing your audience to understanding body language, and from building networks of contacts to using stories

- ■ Examples and lessons from benchmark businesses, including American Express and The Body Shop and ideas from the smartest thinkers, including Naomi Klein, Richard Lewis and Frances Cairncross

- ■ Includes a glossary of key concepts and a comprehensive resources guide

>>EXPRESS EXEC.COM<<
essential management thinking at your fingertips

Copyright © Capstone Publishing 2002

The right of Roger Cartwright to be identified as the author of this work has been asserted in accordance with the Copyright, Designs and Patents Act 1988

First published 2002 by
Capstone Publishing (A Wiley Company)
8 Newtec Place
Magdalen Road
Oxford OX4 1RE
United Kingdom
http://www.capstoneideas.com

All rights reserved. Except for the quotation of short passages for the purposes of criticism and review, no part of this publication may be reproduced, stored in a retrieval system, or transmitted, in any form or by any means, electronic, mechanical, photocopying, recording or otherwise, without the prior permission of the publisher.

CIP catalogue records for this book are available from the British Library and the US Library of Congress

ISBN 1-84112-364-1

This book is printed on acid-free paper

Substantial discounts on bulk quantities of Capstone books are available to corporations, professional associations and other organizations. Please contact Capstone for more details on +44 (0)1865 798 623 or (fax) +44 (0)1865 240 941 or (e-mail) info@wiley-capstone.co.uk

Contents

Introduction to ExpressExec

ExpressExec is 3 million words of the latest management thinking compiled into 10 modules. Each module contains 10 individual titles forming a comprehensive resource of current business practice written by leading practitioners in their field. From brand management to balanced scorecard, ExpressExec enables you to grasp the key concepts behind each subject and implement the theory immediately. Each of the 100 titles is available in print and electronic formats.

Through the ExpressExec.com Website you will discover that you can access the complete resource in a number of ways:

» printed books or e-books;
» e-content – PDF or XML (for licensed syndication) adding value to an intranet or Internet site;
» a corporate e-learning/knowledge management solution providing a cost-effective platform for developing skills and sharing knowledge within an organization;
» bespoke delivery – tailored solutions to solve your need.

Why not visit www.expressexec.com and register for free key management briefings, a monthly newsletter and interactive skills checklists. Share your ideas about ExpressExec and your thoughts about business today.

Please contact elound@wiley-capstone.co.uk for more information.

Introduction to Communication

» At a higher level, social animal communication is vital to human survival as a species.
» Good communication skills are a key component in leadership.
» Communication also involves transmission and feedback.
» Communication occurs using verbal and non-verbal means.

It is common practice when running training sessions on leadership to ask the participants to list the skills and traits that they associate with successful leaders. The writer of this material has never run such a session (and he has been involved with hundreds around the world) without communication skills featuring in the top three or four responses.

This is hardly surprising for, as primates, we are highly social, co-operative animals (despite the impression one may occasionally gain from the news) and, to such a species, effective communication between group members is vital for survival. In social animals, communication also serves to reinforce the structure and tasks of the group – the very conditions that appertain to the world of work and business. Leaders have to do many things in fulfillment of their personal and corporate objectives. They have to:

» motivate
» plan
» resource
» discipline
» control
» evaluate
» set an example.

But to do these things, they have to communicate their vision, their objectives, their plans, and their emotions (e.g. praise) to others. Leadership has two components – the first is visionary and the second is the dissemination of that vision to those whose role it is to carry out the tasks necessary for making the vision a reality. These people need, in turn, to communicate to the leader the demands of each task, their personal requirements, and the progress made in order for plans to be changed in light of circumstances.

It was John Donne, the seventeenth-century English poet, who wrote "No man is an Island, entire of itself; every man is a piece of the Continent, a part of the main."[1] It is communication that prevents us being insular.

As human beings we possess a varied and highly developed communication system, albeit one that fails at times. Not only do we use words but, as will be shown later, we also use intonation, volume, symbols, music, humor, and body language as part of our personal communications fit. The term *communications fit* comes from the military and is used to describe the varied communications equipment fitted to military hardware. If one visits the Boston Naval Yard (or Portsmouth Royal Dockyard in the UK) and goes on board the USS *Constitution* (or HMS *Victory*), it is amazing that the only means the ships had to communicate with other ships was to come close enough to shout or use flags. Examine a photograph of the USS *Normandy* (CG60) and her upper works are a mass of aerials and antenna. Just as military communications have evolved, so have the means by which leaders communicate with their people and the people pass their views on to their leaders.

Despite the obvious importance of communication, it is something we are often quite poor at. We do not always say what we mean and we often do not mean what we say. We rely too much on the spoken word when, as a species, we actually depend on vision 80% of the time. We frequently overlook feelings or cultural nuances in communication. All too often we fail to check that the respondent has actually understood the message. Just asking "Did you understand that?" is of no use. Somebody may well believe that they have understood something when the message was actually quite different. The classic story of misunderstanding a message is the charge of the Light Brigade of British cavalry during the Crimean War in the early 1850s. Nobody ordered them to charge the Russian guns. To the commander-in-chief the message was quite clear – unfortunately he sent it verbally and there was no opportunity to check back. Many lives were lost that day.

This material is designed to assist leaders in ensuring that the message is not only clear to themselves but is also transmitted in such a manner as to remain clear and understandable to respondents, with opportunities for the latter to seek clarification where required.

NOTE

1 Donne, J. (1624) "Meditation XVII", *Devotions upon Emergent Occasions*.

What is Communication?

- » Communication is a key leadership skill.
- » Communication is a two-way process of disseminating vision, ideas, and instructions one way and feedback and evaluation the other.
- » Listening is an important communication skill.
- » Leaders communicate both internally within the organization and externally to the wider society.
- » Spin has become very popular in political circles, but may not fool the audience.
- » Leaders can use the techniques of story-writing and storytelling to improve their communication skills.

"The world will little note, nor long remember what we say here..."

President Abraham Lincoln, Gettysburg, November 19, 1863

Lincoln spoke for less than two minutes at Gettysburg on that November day in the middle of the American Civil War. Before he spoke, the crowd was given a speech that was one hour and fifty-seven minutes long by Edward Everett, former governor of Massachusetts. Nobody appears to have remembered or even recorded what Everett said. Lincoln's short speech has gone down in history and been written about and, later, even recorded by such luminaries as Margaret Thatcher, the British prime minister throughout the 1980s, nicknamed the Iron Lady. What is it about the Gettysburg address that makes it one of history's great pieces of communication?

The Gettysburg address, like many of the great speeches of Winston Spencer Churchill, is short and succinct, and appeals to both the head and the heart. It "does something" to those who are not from the US because it speaks to basic human feelings. It is a brilliant piece of communication, delivered at a difficult time – it offers hope and a better future for the nation.

Great leaders, whether they are in business, politics, religion, or the military, have the ability to communicate – without that ability they would be unable to function as leaders. They say the right thing at the right time, by verbal or non-verbal means. They are always "on message," as the current political phrase would have it. They do not always give the most pleasant of messages, because sometimes that it is impossible, but their message always addresses what people need rather than want to hear.

DEFINING COMMUNICATION

In the context of leadership, communication is the dissemination of the leader's vision, ideas, and instructions to subordinates; the method by which the leader hears the views of subordinates, receives feedback as to their understanding, and obtains an evaluation of projects; the leader's negotiations with those from outside the organization; and the way the leader communicates the vision to the society of which the organization is a part.

Whilst much communication is verbal, either in writing or speech, there is also the non-verbal aspect to consider. Many messages are actually negated or reinforced by body language and attitude. It is just as important that the leader masters non-verbal communication as verbal communication itself. This topic will be discussed further in Chapter 6.

Very large volumes have been written about the mechanics of communication and this material focuses on the part effective communication plays in leadership.

Listening

Perhaps the most important point contained in this material is that communication is not just about talking. Listening is possibly a more vital (certainly a harder) skill than talking or writing. Listening and watching provide the information for any response. Fail to listen and watch, and the response may be inappropriate. Too many people, especially managers, talk for 80% of the time and listen for 20%. They would be more effective if this were the other way around. Just listening to somebody shows this person that their views are respected – an important motivator.

Unfortunately, whilst there are many programs dedicated to public speaking, there appear to be few that deal with the really important topic – public/private listening.

Spin

There has been much written in the media in recent years about the tendency of politicians and others to "spin." Spinning is putting a positive front on what should be a negative message. There are armies of spin doctors in Washington, London, Paris, Tokyo, Moscow, etc. trying to show that nobody ever fails and everything is really A-OK. How different from the dark days of 1940 when, on May 13, Winston Churchill stood up in the House of Commons in London and said: "I have nothing to offer but blood, toil, tears and sweat." That was an occasion when the truth was needed and Churchill, brilliant communicator that he was, realized that no platitudes would do – his country was in dire peril and people needed to know. People not only recognize the truth, but they actually appreciate it, something that many leaders today need to realize.

Are you sitting comfortably?

British children in the 1930s, 1940s, and 1950s, before the days of mass television, had their own slot, *Children's Hour*, on the BBC radio service. The daily story always began with the words "Are you sitting comfortably," usually followed by "Once upon a time."

Stories as a means of communication are as old as the human species. Cultures such as that of the Celts (encompassing Ireland, the West of Scotland, Wales, Cornwall in the UK, Galicia in Northern Spain, and Britanny in France) have had an oral tradition that has survived into the present day. In these cultures storytellers were personages of great importance; they were not just entertainers, but custodians of cultural history and traditions. They acted as a major channel of communication and thus formed an important part of the leader's entourage. Blondel, the faithful servant of King Richard I of England (Richard the Lionheart), who discovered the whereabouts of his imprisoned master on the Continent, then returned to England, and helped raised the ransom money to free him, was not a politician or general but a troubadour and storyteller.

In the New Testament, Jesus Christ uses the story technique to teach his disciples and followers. As they are recorded, these events involved people sitting around Jesus being told parables – stories with a special meaning that taught a moral or religious point. Such techniques are actually highly effective. In the modern world, advertisements that involve a storyline can be particularly effective – the storyline around the Gold Blend couple, used to advertise coffee in both the UK and the US, was so successful that there were advertisements in the national newspapers saying when the next Gold Blend advertisement would appear on television.

What makes a good story?

If storytelling is an important part of communication and if good communication is important to leaders, it is necessary to consider the elements of a good story and to see how they can be transferred into the business world.

It does not matter whether a story is for children or adults, males or females – good stories have the following attributes in common:

» **Believable or permitting the suspension of disbelief.** Take Tom Clancy's series of books that lead from Jack Ryan being a middle-range analyst with the CIA to becoming president of the US. Each book is carefully researched and thus the events by themselves are believable. However that all the things that happen to Ryan could happen to the same person is much less believable. This is where the suspension of disbelief comes in. If the individual event is believable, our brains can suspend our disbelief that such a succession of events could occur and we can enjoy the individual story. In the UK, it has been remarked that if the city of Oxford, setting for the highly popular *Inspector Morse* crime series, experienced the number of murders written about by Colin Dexter, it would be the murder capital of the world rather than the ancient university city it is. Again, disbelief can be suspended because the individual stories are so well crafted.

» **Characterization and identification.** Whoever is listening to the story needs to be able to identify with the feelings of the main characters. They do not have to agree with what the characters do, say, or feel but there must be a degree of empathy.

» **A clear structure.** All of the best stories have a clear structure that leads the listener or reader through the story. Classically this has been an introduction, a main middle section, and a conclusion/ending. However, it is possible to start at the end and work back to (or indeed start at) the middle and then go to the introduction. Check out some good novels to see the type of format used.

» **Accuracy.** Books are often divided up into fiction and non-fiction. However the demarcation is not always as clear as it might seem. Even a work of complete fiction must be set in a historical context, whether the past, the present, or a view of the future. In order that the story is believable this means that the writer must ensure the accuracy of the background, in the same way that the writer of non-fiction must do with their facts. Many fiction writers spend a great deal of time on their research into the background setting of their work. Janet Lawrence, the British writer of crime fiction who uses the Venetian painter Canaletto's time in London as the background to a series in which the painter is the detective, must know as much about London then and about Canaletto's life and works as somebody writing a scholarly thesis. The details must be right or the reader will be turned off the story.

» **Visualization**. A good story promotes a visual image in the mind of the reader or listener. Humans are a highly visual animal, as will be explained in Chapters 3 and 6. One of the advantages of hearing or reading a story, as opposed to seeing it enacted on the TV or movie screen, is that the recipient can build up their own mental picture and contextualize the story in light of their own experiences. This is why the movie of the book often disappoints somebody who has read the book first.

» **Pace and style**. The best story needs to be told in a style and at a pace that suits the recipient. Even non-fiction material should be presented in an agreeable style. As will be covered below, one of the skills of a storyteller is to bring life and animation to mere words on a page.

The contribution of the storyteller

It is believed that of anything that is said, 40% of the understanding comes from the words themselves and 60% from the way they are said. Volume, intonation, etc. play a huge role in human understanding. Take the simple sentence "Come here." This can be said angrily, romantically, in an exasperated manner, with a laugh, or with menace. The two words are in fact capable of multiple meanings, the correct one of which will be provided by the way in which they are said.

As stated in the previous section, the skill of the storyteller is to add life and extra meaning to words - a skill that was once highly prized, declined to a degree, and has been revived due to the popularity of audio books. However, most parents possess the skill and exercise it every time they read their child a story. The effective leader has it as well. Such a person does not just tell - they animate and, most importantly, they involve the recipient. It is no coincidence that many children's stories include the question "And why do you think that was?" - this involves the child in the story and makes them think.

The leader as a storyteller

CEOs of major corporations are not going to gather their executives around them and tell stories and parables, but they can harness the skills of the storyteller to aid understanding. There is no reason why they cannot use allegories to illustrate points. They do not have to speak in monotones. They can adapt what they are saying to aid others to build up a mental picture.

The objective of communication is understanding. A communication that is carefully thought out with both the communicator and the recipient in mind is more likely to be effective than one that just suits the communicator. No one should have to ask, "What did they mean by that?" A leader with good communication skills will have anticipated the question.

The renowned professor Denis McQuail has done much in the academic world to stimulate debate about communication by leaders. His profile can be found in Chapter 8.

KEY LEARNING POINTS

- » Leaders are required to develop excellent communication skills.
- » Listening is as important a skill as talking or writing.
- » The skills of the story-writer and storyteller are useful for leaders.
- » Communication is not just about messages – it also involves feedback.
- » Leaders communicate internally and externally in respect of the organization.

The Evolution of Communication

» Humans are social animals with similar physiology and basic behavior patterns to other primates.
» To humans, as primates, communication skills are important for co-operation and group bonding.
» Non-verbal communication is often more important than verbal communication.
» It is harder to alter body language responses than verbal responses.
» The evolution of communication has been in the areas of speed, distance, and accessibility.

As communication has been a human skill ever since the species evolved (indeed communication evolves as a behavior in the same way as physical characteristics), it is necessary to limit this study of the history of communication to some key issues connected with leadership.

PRIMATE COMMUNICATION

Human beings belong to an animal group known as primates. Containing many of the most advanced mammals, primates have certain key characteristics, many of which are related to eating brightly colored fruits and an arboreal life swinging through trees.

» They can rotate the two bones of the lower arm, the radius and the ulna, over each other and also touch (oppose) their thumb with all the other fingers on the hand. This makes for a very complex joint ideal for grasping branches and twisting, rather than pulling, fruit off trees, or in the case of humans (and to a lesser extent chimpanzees) using increasingly complex tools. Once tools begin to be used, the need for effective communication becomes even greater.
» They have stereoscopic vision - important for gauging distance and color vision - which is useful if you eat brightly colored fruits and use tools, as such tasks requires hand-eye co-ordination and accuracy.
» Primates are social animals normally living in fairly large groups. Thus, an effective means of communication between group members is necessary for co-operation and maintaining group bonds.
» Primates are highly intelligent.
» Primate groups are highly structured and hierarchical. Leadership is a fundamental survival requirement for such groups.

Humans have over 90% of their genetic material in common with other higher primates. It is no surprise that the behavior of chimpanzees, gorillas, etc. intrigues us so much, as we can often see reflections of our own actions in it. Desmond Morris, the anthropologist, broadcaster, writer, and ex-curator of London Zoo, has shown how the leadership qualities and communication techniques of humans are mirrored by other primate societies. In his work *The Human Zoo* he compared the ten most important rules of leadership and dominance in primate societies and argued that they applied equally to all leaders, from baboons to modern presidents and prime ministers.[1]

Whether we like it or not, it would appear that much of our behavior has its roots in our shared primate ancestry and the manner in which we communicate appears to be no different. One of the reasons we are so intrigued by the way other primates behave is that, when watching them, we have a perhaps greater understanding of what they feel than with any other type of animal, as their expressions and gestures are so like our own.

LANGUAGE

Humans are not unique in possessing language, but the complexity of the language of even the most primitive human society is far, far greater than that of any other species. There is no doubt that marine mammals of the whale family use sound to communicate in a semi-conversational manner, whilst bees use a visual dance to pass on complex directions to other bees. Humans, however, have developed languages that are both functional and rich in emotional complexities. Human communication is not all verbal though.

As humans spread over the globe, so different languages developed. Many languages are related to each other. Western European languages often have the roots of their words in Latin. English, the most common international language of communication, has roots in Latin, German, and French as well as the original Anglo-Saxon. There are similarities between Spanish and Italian or between the Nordic languages. One of the strangest similarities is that between Turkish and Finnish, two countries at different extremes of Europe/Asia.

Within languages, dialects develop and with them accents. Whilst many Britons may sound the same to somebody from the US, Britons can often spot the region of the UK that somebody comes from by their accent. Those in the US can do the same with their accents, New England and Georgia having a quite different sound. Throughout much of the twentieth century, there was a tendency in the UK to try to eliminate regional variation and have everybody speaking what is termed received pronunciation (otherwise known as the Queen's English or BBC English). This trend has passed and regional variation is welcomed as it adds variety. There have also been attempts recently, especially within Europe, to revive ancient languages such as Welsh, Gaelic, Breton, and Catalan. Many of these were repressed for political reasons in order to bring their speakers into the mainstream of the larger nation. There is now a realization that language variation does not always imply separatism.

In the US there are a number of languages spoken. Whilst English is the most widely used, Spanish is also spoken by many – as are Chinese, Yiddish, and the Native American languages. Countries such as India that have a large number of indigenous languages often adopt an official language for trade and business purposes – in the case of India it is English.

The oldest language preserved in writing, Sumerian, was written in cuneiform script. Its earliest records date from about 3000 BC; after about 2000 BC it was no longer spoken, but it continued in use as a literary language until cuneiform writing died out in about the first century BC. Today, many languages use a Roman-style script, most Slavonic languages use Cyrillic, Arabic uses a cursive script, and some east Asian languages use a script based on pictorial symbols (pictograms).

The natural eye movements of a baby are from right to left – the way Arabic and some Asian languages are written. Users of languages such as English that run left to right have to train their eyes to do this naturally.

NON-VERBAL COMMUNICATION

Konrad Lorenz showed how easy it was to tell whether a dog was angry or not by looking at the position of its ears. Lorenz studied aggression and his work *On Aggression* is a classic.[2] The fact is that many of the messages we communicate to one another are, like the ears of the dog, highly visual. A person saying something pleasant but with a scowl on their face is likely to have the scowl believed over the pleasant words. As animals we are instinctively programmed to react to such visual, body-language clues and they take precedent over other messages. The importance of the polygraph in legal proceedings is that the vast majority of people have no way of controlling the nerve impulses that it records. The same is true of body language. If a person is uncomfortable in a situation, that discomfort will show through in their stance and facial expression, no matter how much they deny it. One of the great skills of acting, the reason for "getting into a part," is the ability to act out the body language so that the audience actually believes that the performer is feeling what they are saying. Whilst body language has been something that everybody knows about and understands on an instinctive basis, it was not really studied until researchers such as Lorenz began to delve into human behavior. Body language is fairly universal amongst humans, but there are cultural differences. Nodding the head is not a universal sign of agreement: in some Asian cultures it is more a sign of understanding than of agreement and in Southern India it is less of a nod and more of a shake - making conversations somewhat difficult for those from the West for whom a shake means "no." Signs of agreement such as "thumbs up" are offensive in some cultures, as they have sexual connotations. However anger, smiles, confidence, fear, etc. appear to be universal in their manifestation. A good leader needs to recognize the body language of others and work on their own. As Desmond Morris has pointed out, a leader who shows signs of fear or a lack of confidence may be on their way out. The public face of leadership is more about body language than words.[3]

In addition to personal body language, the writer of this material and his colleague George Green have developed the concept of organizational body language (OBL), which refers to the messages an organization puts out about its culture and relationships by the way its facilities and other features are designed.[4] It is often easy to see who is the most important, the staff or the customers, by examining the parking lot arrangements. If the customers have to walk a long way in the rain to reach reception, this is indicative of how much their needs have been considered.

SYMBOLS AND SOUNDBITES

Symbols

In their work on corporate strategy, Gerry Johnson and Kevin Scholes noted the importance of symbols as part of what they termed the cultural web of an organization.[5]

Humans have used symbols since the earliest days of cave painting. The ancient Egyptian hieroglyphs were a mixture of writing and symbolic representation. The Christian Cross and the Red Cross (and its Islamic equivalent, the Red Crescent) of history have been joined by the Nike "Swoosh" and the Shell patina in being recognized throughout the world. Symbols have often carried with them more than just a pragmatic indication of a function – they have come to represent a set of values. Thus one does not see a Red Cross symbol and think purely "hospital" but also of care, refuge, safety, freedom from attack, etc. This is one reason why many people become inflamed when an attack is made on a building carrying such a symbol, as the attack becomes an attack on their values.

Commercial logos and brand names have become so important in representing the product and its company that it is often they that carry the value of the organization. Naomi Klein, who has studied this area in detail, reports that in 1988 Philip Morris paid not $2.1bn for Kraft (the actual worth of the company) but $12.6bn (the worth of the company plus the Kraft name)![6] For a profile of Klein, see Chapter 8.

Soundbites

A recent phenomenon that may well be the verbal equivalent of a symbol is the soundbite. Developed for television audiences, the soundbite is a short piece of material that encapsulates a more complex idea. Many have been regarded as trite but some have gone down in history to be reproduced in dictionaries of quotations, for example Franklin D. Roosevelt's famous line in his first inaugural address in 1933, "I pledge you, I pledge myself, to a new deal for the American people." The expression New Deal eventually became applied to a whole raft of social and economic policies during Roosevelt's record number of terms of office. Soundbites can be effective rallying calls just as flags, one of the most potent symbols of all, are. Think of the values and traditions represented by the Stars and Stripes or the Union flag and one can understand the power of such non-verbal symbols. The image of the US Marines raising the flag on the Japanese island of Iwo Jima in 1945 speaks to the emotions far more eloquently than any number of descriptive words.

PRINTING

The importance of the written word really grew after a means was found to make it more accessible. Whether printing is an Eastern or Western invention is a matter of conjecture – that our lives would be very different without printing is not.

Movable metal type was first cast in Europe and printed on paper with a printing press by the middle of the fifteenth century. The invention appears to have been unrelated to earlier developments in the Far East, where the techniques differed considerably in detail. The earliest Western printers in the Rhine River valley used mechanical presses derived in design from wine presses and made of wood. Printers developed a technique of casting types with such precision that the letters could be held together by pressure applied to the edges of the tray containing the type for the page. In this system, a single letter a fraction of a millimeter too big could cause the letters surrounding it to fall out of the page. The development of a method of casting letters to precise dimensions was the essential contribution of the Western invention. Johannes Gutenberg, of the German city of Mainz, is traditionally considered the inventor of Western printing in about 1450.

The art of papermaking, introduced into the West in the twelfth century, spread throughout Europe in the thirteenth and fourteenth centuries. By the mid-fifteenth century, paper was available in abundance – it was no use having a technique without the necessary ancillary materials, in this case the paper to print on. During the Renaissance, the rise of a prosperous and literate middle class increased the demand for quantities of reading matter. The emergence of Martin Luther, the success of the Reformation, and the subsequent spread of religious wars were heavily dependent on the printing press and on the steady stream of printed pamphlets, the pen proving mightier than the sword from an early date.

There were those in authority who did not agree with the dissemination of the printed word. In a later era, they would object to the railways for the same reasons – books put too much knowledge into the hands of the lower orders and the railways allowed them to move. The printed page more than any other invention speeded the movement of ideas.

Printing techniques have changed beyond all recognition, but the power of the written word has not. Books were once a luxury; now, in the developed world, they are a normal part of daily life. Much of the world's population has access to newspapers and the news and ideas that they feature. Despite concerns that television would harm reading habits, the opposite appears to have happened. There are 1.5 million books in print at any one time in English alone and book sales are at an all-time high – over $38bn in the US in 2000.

The availability of books and newspapers also led to a rise in literacy and education. This opened up leadership possibilities for many and began a process of breaking down previous social hierarchies. Anybody who could read could gain both knowledge and ideas, and from the ranks of the working and middle classes came leaders empowered by the written word – none more so than in the US.

DISTANCE

Imperial Rome had a postal service, as did the earlier Egyptian dynasties, but it was not until the invention of the postage stamp that ordinary people were able to make regular use of mail services. The first American postal service was established in the colony of Massachusetts in 1639. From 1707 until the year before the American Revolution, the General Post Office in London controlled the postal service in America. In 1775 the Continental Congress resolved to have a postal system of its own, and Benjamin Franklin was elected to carry on the work. When a US postal service was authorized by Congress under the Constitution in 1789, the nation had 75 local post offices and the mail was carried over 1875 miles of postal routes.

In 1840, the British politician Roland Hill introduced the first penny post service, by which a letter could be sent from any part of the UK to any other for one penny. Prior to that, distance had been the determiner of cost, with letters from London to Scotland costing over one shilling (twelve pence). Furthermore the recipient, not the sender, paid – a method that would cause uproar in today's world of junk and unsolicited mail! As with books, a cheap mail service allowed ideas as well as news to move quickly over long distances.

Next came the telegraph, necessary to regulate railway movements, soon to be followed by the telephone and later the radio. As with all such inventions the telephone was first a toy of the rich, but today most people in the developed world have at least one home telephone and often a mobile one as well.

Keeping in touch is a key function of leaders and it has become progressively easier to do so – sometimes too easy as leaders and subordinates can end up suffering from information overload.

ELECTRONICS

The introduction of the Internet and computers has brought a whole new dimension to communication. Whilst the computer revolution has brought dramatic changes to the way people and businesses communicate, these changes are in fact evolutionary. The history of communication has been one of moving information quicker over longer distances and involving more and more people. This is such an important subject for today's business leaders that it is covered as a separate chapter – see Chapter 4. The evolution of communication, from the development of writing to the information age, is represented as a timeline in Fig. 3.1.

KEY LEARNING POINTS

» Humans share much of their genetic inheritance with other primates, to whom communication between group members is very important.

» The development of accessible means of communication allows more people to become leaders, as they have both knowledge and a medium for their ideas.

» Leaders should never neglect non-verbal communication: it is as important as verbal communication.

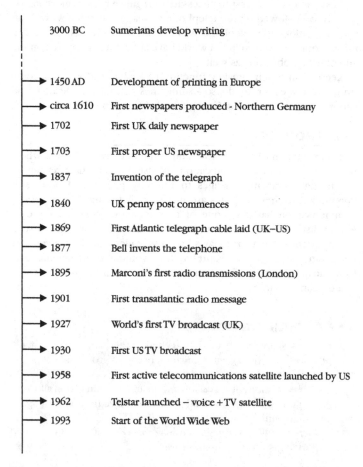

3000 BC	Sumerians develop writing	
1450 AD	Development of printing in Europe	
circa 1610	First newspapers produced - Northern Germany	
1702	First UK daily newspaper	
1703	First proper US newspaper	
1837	Invention of the telegraph	
1840	UK penny post commences	
1869	First Atlantic telegraph cable laid (UK–US)	
1877	Bell invents the telephone	
1895	Marconi's first radio transmissions (London)	
1901	First transatlantic radio message	
1927	World's first TV broadcast (UK)	
1930	First US TV broadcast	
1958	First active telecommunications satellite launched by US	
1962	Telstar launched – voice + TV satellite	
1993	Start of the World Wide Web	

Fig. 3.1 A timeline showing the evolution of communication over some 5000 years.

NOTES

1 Morris, D. (1969) *The Human Zoo*. Jonathan Cape, London.
2 Lorenz, K. (1966) *On Aggression*. Methuen, London.
3 Morris, *The Human Zoo, op. cit.*
4 Cartright, R. and Green, R. (1997) *In Charge of Customer Satisfaction*. Blackwell, Oxford.
5 Johnson, G. and Scholes, K. (1984) *Exploring Corporate Strategy*. Prentice Hall, Hemel Hempstead.
6 Klein, N. (2000) *No Logo: No space, no choice, no jobs, taking aim at the brand bullies*. Flamingo, London.

The E-Dimension of Communication

» The Internet allows for real-time conversations irrespective of distance.
» Face-to-face meetings may still be important, especially until people get to know each other.
» Even with videoconferencing, body language clues may be indistinct.
» Protocols are needed to avoid curtness.
» Do not use the Internet if the person is near to you.

As organizations become more and more global in their operations, staff need to be managed across an increasingly large geographic area. The effects of the global dimension to modern leadership, and the implications for communication skills and systems, form the subject of the next chapter. This chapter concentrates on the use of the Internet and electronic communications for the leadership function, whilst the next chapter centers on the general communication skills of the global leader.

THE INTERNET

The Internet began with the linking together of a series of computers in the Advanced Research Projects Agency (ARPA) of the US Department of Defense to form what became known in 1969 as ARPANET. This network was designed to protect military communications in the event of a nuclear attack – a very real fear in the cold war political climate of the time. The system used three university hosts in California and one in Utah. Later, in the 1970s, the US academic community set up a purely civilian network funded by the National Science Foundation (NSF), which linked an increasing number of US and foreign universities via NSFNET. For the first time academics and researchers could communicate text via a new medium known as electronic mail, which rapidly became contracted to the acronym e-mail.

As students who had used e-mail began to take up positions within the private sector it was not long before large commercial organizations in the US, beginning with computer companies such as IBM and Hewlett-Packard, began to talk to each other via e-mail linking their systems to NSFNET.

In 1993 Marc Andreessen and his group at the University of Illinois introduced the first Web browser, Mosaic, a software application for the UNIX operating system, which was later adapted for Apple Macintosh and Microsoft Windows. NSFNET gradually became less relevant and the commercial world saw the birth of Internet service providers (ISPs), so that by the middle of the 1990s organizations in both the public and private sectors were not only using e-mail but were beginning to design and post Web pages. By 1993, the World Wide Web (WWW) had been born.

For non-computer specialists, one of the main implications of the Internet has been for communication. For organizations, the Internet and e-mail have revolutionized both internal and external communication. The power of information and communication technology (ICT) is less in the attributes of the individual components – computers, telephones, radio transmitters, cameras, etc. – but in the synergy that can be obtained when they are used in conjunction with each other and linked together in a network. ICT has provided leaders with almost instantaneous contact with members of their team, no matter how far away those members may be. The contact is almost instantaneous because team members are human and need to eat and sleep, and so cannot be available for communication 24 hours per day as the computer can be.

FACE-TO-FACE AND REMOTE COMMUNICATION

Even videoconferencing is an imprecise medium for passing on body language clues to the recipient, for reasons described below. The four typologies of communication are shown in Fig. 4.1. The titles of each segment are designed to be indicative of the type of communication.

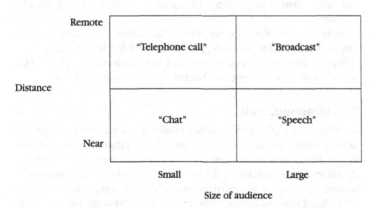

Fig. 4.1 Four typologies of communication represented in terms of speaker-listener distance and audience size.

The chat

The chat is the most intimate form of communication, being conducted either one to one or in a small group. It may be formal or informal, between equals or initiated by either the subordinate or the leader. As all parties can see each other, they are able to assess not only the words spoken but also the non-verbal body language clues that accompany them. Provided that there is as much listening as there is talking (see Chapter 2), this can be the most productive type of communication. If the listening element is minimized the "chat" becomes an argument, and arguments are seldom if ever productive, often leaving all parties angry and less prone to compromise.

The speech

Again face to face but to a much larger audience. There is less opportunity for feedback and discussion, although the experienced presenter will use the body language of those members of the audience who can be seen as a feedback mechanism. Slight smiles or nods of the head are good indicators that the message is getting across. Hitler was a great exponent of the speech and used his voice to produce hysteria in his listeners. Unfortunately he chose to put his skills to the use of evil rather than good. Perhaps his opposite is the US evangelist Billy Graham.

As both the chat and the speech are conducted with parties in close physical contact, the technological aspects are likely to be simple and related to microphones or audio-visual aids. However, with the more remote typologies, technology begins to play a more vital role.

The telephone call

A traditional telephone call can be thought of as a letter in real time. The development, and growth in the use, of the facsimile (fax) machine in the 1980s was in fact just that – a real-time method of sending a document. Written material does not allow for the easy transmission of feelings, although it is a permanent record. The telephone call on the other hand does allow for some expression, although voices may be distorted. More than one operation involving selling over the telephone has "smile as you dial" displayed in big letters for the sales staff because, just as eyes can pick up body language clues, our ears can detect the difference in speech patterns of somebody who is smiling or not. This is because different muscle groups are used and these alter the tone of voice.

E-mail, the latest alternative to the telephone, for all its uses tends to be a very curt method of communication. There are protocols for expressing emotion but the use of symbols for a smile has nowhere near the impact of an actual smile. There has also been an issue as to the number of e-mails people receive. It is so easy to send a copy to all the people on a mailing list, but is it really necessary to e-mail the person next to you?

The use of videoconferencing as a device to link sites has grown rapidly in recent years, aided by the availability of PCs with cameras using Windows software and operating through the Internet. However, even with the best definition available, the body language clues are hard to pick up. The pixel definition of even the most expensive technology is nowhere near as good as the human eye. There tends always to be a minute time lag between sites and this further confuses the interpretation of the visual clues.

Where the Internet has proved to be a boon is in the area of corporate dissemination and the ability to form diverse multifunctional teams. Colin Hastings and his colleagues in the UK have stressed the importance of managing "the team apart" in their work on superteams.[1] ICT can help ensure that all members of a team or project group are as well informed as possible about developments, as will be described in the case study at the end of this chapter.

The broadcast

Videoconferencing as described above or audio-conferencing can be used to address large groups. The former does allow for basic feedback, whilst only roars of approval or disapproval (or stunned silence) are available using the latter. Nevertheless they do provide means by which the leader of a large group can address those listening. Broadcasts by leaders and politicians have long been used to provide reassurance or reports – the annual state-of-the-nation report by the US president or the British monarch's Christmas broadcast in the UK are examples. Such communications are unfortunately one-way and thus do not provide for any meaningful feedback.

COMMUNICATION AND THE LEADER IN THE TWENTY-FIRST CENTURY

Global aspects of leadership and communication are the subject of the next chapter, but it is worth stressing here the point made by Black, Morrison, and Gregersen in their study *Global Explorers*.[2] They quote a manager of an oil company who emphasizes the need to communicate the leader's competence and priorities very quickly. Obviously a face-to-face meeting with the team is the best way to do this. In the case study below, a face-to-face meeting was the first step in the development of a project, but this is not always possible. As will be shown in the next chapter, the leader needs to use all the means of communication at their disposal to ensure that not only their priorities, but also their vision and means of operating, are communicated to all who need to know. Whatever means of communicating are used, the leader needs to remember that they are telling a story and that explanation plus instruction plus consequences will always be more effective than just an instruction.

CASE STUDY ILLUSTRATING BEST PRACTICE: THE UHI

Given the importance of face-to-face contact, including an ability to use body language to gain clues about real thinking, it is not surprising that the use of the Internet is at an early stage when it comes to managing and leading staff. It is doubtful whether any present court or tribunal would look kindly upon the hiring or firing of staff purely by e-mail, although doubtless that day will come. There are organizations, however, where the staff are so widely scattered that the sheer geography of the situation makes the use of electronic communications not just useful but a key part of the organizations' ability to function and survive, and the only method team leaders have for regular contact with their teams.

One such organization is the University of the Highlands and Islands (UHI) in Scotland, set up in the 1990s to link the further education colleges in the north of Scotland (plus a number of specialist institutions). The UHI now has over 20 sites stretching from the Shetland Islands in the north, through the newly designated city of Inverness at the mouth of Loch Ness to the ancient capital of Scotland, Perth, further south and the island of Lewis in the west. With hundreds of staff in support, technical, and academic roles, the UHI has only a small central staff at its executive office; most staff being out in the colleges. These institutions retain their independence whilst being part of a federal university. Students can study close to home without having to travel miles across sometimes difficult terrain. Technology is being used to obviate the need for staff to travel. The way the UHI manages such a diverse staff is covered as a case study in the *Managing Diversity* title in this series.[3] This study concerns the leadership of a particular team spread across the full range of northern Scotland in the late 1990s.

The UHI has its own dedicated telephone system that is used for both telephone and visual communication. Much use is made of videoconferencing via a multi-link system that allows multiple sites to videoconference with each other. The whole system uses an integrated services digital network – in this case ISDN 6 – ensuring the highest possible quality of visual reproduction. In addition to the main videoconference suites on the component sites, increasing numbers of staff have video cameras attached to their personal computers, enabling them to videoconference from their desk using Windows software.

An important objective for the UHI is to ensure that all staff feel a sense of ownership and belonging. The videoconferencing and e-mail (using GroupWise) is used for staff communication, teaching, and tutorials. Despite the body language problems mentioned earlier in this chapter, the technology has proved beneficial in bringing staff together without the need to travel. There are no freeways or motorways north of Perth and the main roads are mainly single-carriageway, with the few railways there are being (with one exception) single-track. Air travel saves time but is very expensive. A full-fare ticket from Aberdeen to the Shetland Islands can cost as much as a special offer London-to-New York flight. Thus travel can be very long and time-wasting, as well as being a major expense. For staff to be able to meet electronically has been important for building the team spirit necessary to meet common goals and objectives, and for carrying out the team leader's managerial functions.

The management development program

An early need for the UHI portfolio was a management development program, available on a part-time basis and at a post-experience level for managers and potential managers. Such a program can be validated by the Institute of Management (UK) and, to the UHI managers considering the issue, this seemed a useful link to make, one that would add credibility to the award of a certificate or diploma for one or two years' study respectively.

The initial partners in the program were from Perth, Inverness, and the islands of Lewis and Orkney. In 1998 interested parties met in Inverness for a two-day meeting, which was also attended by the Institute of Management and a representative of the UHI central office function. Once it was decided to progress, the course leader based at Perth had to manage and develop a team that was not necessarily of his choosing. The vast majority of UHI staff are appointed to a partner institution that then deploys them on UHI programs with the agreement of the UHI faculty leader and the relevant course leader. In this case there were no problems with the staff selected by the partners. The UHI has a vigorous program-reporting mechanism as part of its quality-assurance procedures. This means that course-team reports must be made on a regular basis – course-team meetings are a requirement of this process.

In order to keep the price charged to students at a level that would encourage maximum access, it was necessary to cut down on superfluous costs, especially those of travel. The management program was one of the UHI's first fully networked programs where students would attend seminars at their nearest center or study using distance-learning materials or a combination of both.

The first step in managing the team was for those present at Inverness to take on board development tasks and report back via e-mail to the other members. The team leader then drew the ideas together and submitted the draft proposal to the team for their agreement. It was decided early on that team members must be involved in the whole process, as professionally they were all equals.

The validation process with the Institute of Management was a formal face-to-face event, although subsequent programs have used videoconferencing for such events. Thereafter the team met face to face on only one or two occasions per year, usually at the residential period held for students and at a special development event. All team meetings were undertaken by videoconference with documents being displayed on screen if required. It was these meetings, and a series of experimental videoconferenced seminars for the whole cohort of program students across the network, that highlighted the problem of a body language time lag when videoconferencing. This required some getting used to as it removed some of the clues that body language usually provides about true feelings. The system used was one whereby whoever was speaking gained control of the network – this required meetings to be well chaired and disciplined. All other communication was by e-mail with team members becoming quite chatty. Communication also serves to strengthen team bonds and this approach was encouraged.

The program was well received by students and the Institute of Management. Evaluation after year 1 showed that no team member felt excluded by distance. As the program changed in year 2, due to an alteration in the syllabus, all changes were made using the e-mail and videoconferencing facilities. Again the process was smooth and the team bonds strengthened.

Whilst it is good to meet face to face, on a program such as this it is not always possible financially. The decision to meet at least once per year was an objective one, which recognized that not all team development could be virtual. Especially in the early stages it was important that the members met in the flesh – thereafter it became less important.

The UHI Website can be found at www.uhi.ac.uk

KEY LEARNING POINTS

» The Internet is a useful tool for communication, if used wisely.
» The Internet is good for words and still pictures, but less suitable for communicating feelings.
» Leaders should always try to meet face to face with their staff at least once.

NOTES

1 Hastings, C., Bixby, R., and Chaudhry-Lawton, R. (1994) *Superteams*. Harper Collins, London.
2 Black, J.S., Morrison, A.J., and Gregersen, H.B. (1999) *Global Explorers*. Routledge, New York.
3 Cartwright, R. (2001) *Managing Diversity*. Capstone, Oxford.

The Global Dimension of Communication

» Global communication is technically much easier than in previous times, but cultural sensitivity needs to be observed.
» The global leader needs to ensure that they are aware of how things are done in other places and of what will, and will not, cause misunderstanding and embarrassment.
» Knowledge of the language and stories of an area and culture will greatly aid understanding and provide a reference point for both parties.
» Global communication requires a blend of technical, linguistic, and cultural skills.

In 1982, Brigadier Jeremy Moore of the Royal Marines, commander of the British landing force during the Falklands conflict, spent hours on a satellite communications link at his San Carlos HQ in conversation with London. As Max Hastings and Simon Jenkins have commented, in a previous era a frigate captain would have a sword in one hand, a bible in another, and instructions on his desk that had been issued weeks, months, or even years earlier.[1] Leaders had not the access to the instant communications that they have today. There have been a number of authorities who have stated that the attack on Goose Green that cost Colonel H. Jones his life would never have been launched without the urgent instructions from London delivered instantaneously over the satellite link. Anecdotally, General (later President) Ulysses S. Grant is reputed to have sent a message to Washington during the American Civil War in which he said, "Unless I hear to the contrary within 24 hours I will attack," knowing full well it would take at least three days before a reply could be received. Instant communications can be a curse as well as a blessing.

As discussed in the previous chapter, there is hardly a part of the world where a person cannot be reached or reach others. Mobile telephones increasingly work across the globe and cybercafés allow e-mail messages to be collected and sent from almost anywhere. Today's leaders are never out of touch, which may be a bad rather than a good thing. Leaders are human and need rest and relaxation in the same way as anybody else. A good leader should be able to delegate to a subordinate and forget about their leadership role for a while – leaders are also fathers and mothers, sons and daughters. A happy family life, however it is defined in a pluralist society, is a necessity for psychological well-being. The need for loving relationships (be they different- or same-sex relationships) has been recognized as a key factor in human well-being for many years. Those who are constantly in touch with work cannot at the same time devote time to their relationships. Paradoxically it is both work and home that suffer. The worker becomes burnt out and his or her relationships suffer, so the essential domestic support mechanism may be weakened. There is certainly good sense in the idea of taking a vacation *sans* computer, and *sans* mobile telephone!

THE COMMUNICATION SKILLS OF A GLOBAL LEADER

As more and more organizations become global in their operations, so their leaders and managers need to take a global perspective. As this occurs there is a need to ensure that their communication skills are those necessary to communicate on a global, rather than a local, basis. The story that is being told may have different connotations somewhere else and it is important that the leader has done their homework. These skills fall into three categories:

» technical
» linguistic
» cultural.

Technical communication skills

As the previous chapter demonstrated, the technical aspects of communication have been increasing rapidly. A leader needs to be competent not only at using the basic technology but also at using it to its best advantage. To do this means choosing the most appropriate medium of communication. A rebuke is easy to compose and write as an e-mail, but much harder for the recipient to accept in such an impersonal and curt format – perhaps if a rebuke cannot be delivered face to face, then a letter or the telephone is a better option? As will be shown later, in some cultures curt messages are considered the height of rudeness. Indeed, these and other cultural aspects form an important part of the communication process.

Linguistic communication skills

Arthur Bedeian quotes the case of a manager at Pace Foods Inc. who was highly successful because he spoke Spanish. The company's plant at San Antonio had 75% of its workforce with Spanish as their first language and his ability gained him immediate credibility.[2]

Those for whom English is their first language have been notorious for not learning foreign languages. When the international language of business and transportation is your own, it may seem unnecessary to learn another one. However nothing breaks the ice like a greeting in a person's own language. Not only does speaking a language aid communication with those for whom it is their natural tongue, but it also provides an insight into their way of life. It is almost impossible to learn a language without gaining a knowledge of those who speak it. More and more companies are beginning to insist on competence in another language for senior appointments.

Where the leader does not speak the language (and few, if anybody, can master all of the common languages), then translators are required. It is always a good idea to check written translations carefully. Meanings can become distorted in translation, as is often shown by the translation of notices in foreign hotels. Perhaps one of the classics read: "The bed can accommodate two but by special arrangement room can be made for three." In reality this meant that a spare bed could be fitted into the room for a third person. Have a translator make the first pass and then a native speaker correct any distortions; it can save misunderstandings or even embarrassment.

If the leader's language skills are not good then they should stick to basic greetings and civilities - it is worse to say the wrong thing, or to make a language sound silly, than to say nothing.

Cultural communication skills

Different cultures have different styles of communication. Culture is a reflection of the values and traditions of a society, in effect "the way we do things around here." As organizations have become more global in nature, much effort has been put into developing cultural sensitivity amongst those who will be working and communicating with employees and other people from different cultures. Amongst the leading authorities in this area are Fons Trompenaars, Richard D. Lewis, Philip Harris, and Robert Moran. They have produced excellent guides on how to do business and work with those from other cultures, details of which are provided in other titles in this series and in Chapters 8 and 9 of this material.

As regards communication skills, some examples of the issues that arise have been taken from the studies mentioned above and are summarized below. (Note: there is always a danger of generalization and stereotyping. None of the examples below should be regarded as judgmental. Just because somebody does something differently to you does not mean it is better or worse – it is just different.)

» Standing with one's back to somebody is very rude in Arab culture.
» Gesturing is a common and integral part of communication in Latin and Arab cultures.
» In the Far East, the handing over of business cards is a formal event to be treated with courtesy – the cards should be studied.
» Japanese language contains more nuances than English.
» A direct approach in Japan may be considered rude.
» The Japanese may prevaricate because they don't want to appear rude by saying an outright no.
» Initial pleasantries are very important when communicating with the Chinese.
» Northern Europeans and North Americans prefer a direct, business-like approach to communication.

The examples above are the types of area that a leader needs to study before communicating. As communication is a two-way process, the other party should also acquaint themselves with the method of communicating in the leader's culture. Imagine a communication between a business person from Chicago and one from Beijing. The former will wish to get straight to the point, the latter will be asking about the former's family and state of health. If both know how the other prefers to behave, they can adapt their communication accordingly.

The authorities listed above have provided details covering a large number of countries and should be consulted before attempting to communicate on a global basis.

TRAINING

Before sending staff to work in other countries, many organizations now provide training and awareness programs. These will nearly always include a section on the required communication skills. It is not just the employees who may need assistance; partners, spouses, and other family members may also be involved. In many cultures, these people are expected to play a part in business life and will thus need to be culturally sensitive.

REFERENCE POINTS AND STORIES

One of the problems with global communication is a lack of reference points. This is perhaps less of a problem today than it was, say, 200 years ago when people in different parts of the world might have little in common and few if any shared experiences. A reference point is the common ground that promotes the mutual understanding of communication. Global products such as Coca-Cola, Nike sportswear, Ford cars, Sony Walkmans, and Boeing airplanes might provide a reference point but stories, especially where they are shared between cultures as many are, provide an excellent reference point as they can be used as examples in the communication process. Most cultures and religions have a similar creation story and almost all have a version of the Flood, so as to suggest that something of the kind must, almost certainly, have happened. These provide a basis for common understanding. Within the English-speaking world, the stories of Charles Dickens, Washington Irving, Sir Arthur Conan Doyle, Mark Twain, and William Shakespeare provide considerable common ground, told as they are by parents and schoolteachers from Los Angeles to New York and London to Sydney.

In putting forward vision, policies, and practices the leader needs to ensure that not only are the correct words used but that they are placed in a context that the recipient can relate to as part of their culture. The success of many of the great writers of the world is that they could do just that – they could be enjoyed by anybody because they dealt with basic human emotions and issues.

Television and the movies have greatly aided this process, as they provide a snapshot of other cultures and their way of doing things. They do not run classes on the US legal system in the UK, but when this writer was involved in a legal campaign in New England (not, one hastens to add, as a defendant) the novels of John Grisham and the TV series *LA Law* and *Perry Mason* meant that he had a fairly good idea of the generalities, if not the specifics, of what was happening.

CASE STUDY ILLUSTRATING BEST PRACTICE: RUPERT MURDOCH/NEWS INTERNATIONAL

In August 1993 *Business Week* described the Australian-born media tycoon Rupert Murdoch as "an apostle of global communication who is a master of not telling the world what he really thinks." That Murdoch has mastered the art of global communication cannot be denied. He controls newspapers in the US, the UK (including *The Times*), and Australia. His publishing empire includes Harper-Collins, whilst he is heavily involved in entertainment and satellite broadcasting (Twentieth Century Fox, British Sky Broadcasting, and the LA Dodgers to name but three enterprises that he owns or part-owns), and has a number of Internet-related activities.

Murdoch, born in 1931 to a newspaper-owning family, has acquired some of the most important and prestigious titles and taken on the UK trade unions and won. According to Stuart Crainer, whose *Business the Rupert Murdoch Way* provides a fascinating insight into the man, part of his success has been his development of a network of contacts.[3] Only an excellent global communicator can develop a global network. Crainer quotes many who are terrified of Murdoch's power, but there are also those who admire his method of doing business.

Much of Murdoch's power comes from his ability to keep his finger on the pulse of his operations on an almost constant basis. His managers are used to him contacting them for details of their area of operation at almost any time of the day or night. As a person involved in the global mass communication business, Murdoch makes impressive use of his global personal communication systems. Crainer comments that Murdoch is fed on a diet of quantitative and qualitative information from around his empire. The very process of acquiring, sifting, analyzing, and then using such information on a large scale requires excellent communication skills and the ability to set up a communication network to suit one's own method of working and yet such that others can use it effectively.

To be an effective leader one not only has to create a vision, but also to ensure that it is implemented by employees and others, which means communicating it to other people. Murdoch does not appear to have a formal means of communicating his vision, but it is obviously communicated through the workforce as the high degree of senior executive loyalty reported by Crainer shows.

Given that Murdoch's political views are ambivalent (in the UK he has supported both the Conservative and Labour Parties in print and has behaved in a similar way in Australia), staff need to try to understand the man rather than his beliefs. His overriding principle seems to be that in business he will act in a way that benefits the company. How he votes (he is now a US, not an Australian, citizen) only Rupert Murdoch knows.

Crainer claims that Murdoch is the "consummate communicator" and is successful because he has carried out the type of cultural analysis suggested earlier in this chapter. He understands the people of the regions his companies serve, because he has made it his business to understand how to reach them. Murdoch has commented on how difficult it is to communicate with everybody and to keep his finger on every pulse, but he claims to make a conscious effort to ensure that he can see as much of the total picture as possible. People sometimes refer to this as a business instinct, but it is really using one's communication system to ensure that the organization is in a position to act swiftly when the opportunity arises.

To operate such a global communication empire means that communication use must be high up the leadership agenda. Perhaps a measure of Murdoch's ability to communicate is the number of people outside of his organization who know his name – most CEOs are known only to suppliers and employees – Murdoch is different.

KEY LEARNING POINTS

» Global leaders require more than basic communication skills: they need to be technically, linguistically, and culturally aware.
» Whilst basic human behavior is similar the world over, cultural differences mean that communication processes need to be adapted from area to area.

> › The time taken to learn about people, their language, culture, and stories will not be wasted as it aids communication.
> » Effective communication needs the common ground of a reference point for all the parties involved.

NOTES

1 Hastings, M. and Jenkins, S. (1983) *The Battle for the Falklands*. Michael Joseph, London.
2 Bedeian, A. (1993) *Management*. Harcourt Brace, Orlando.
3 Crainer, S. (1998) *Business the Rupert Murdoch Way*. Capstone, Oxford.

The State of the Art in Communication

» Communication is the passing on of information, ideas, feelings, etc. to another party.
» It may be in the form of words, pictures, music, or gestures.
» Coding and decoding convert thoughts into a "language" that can be transmitted.
» Noise can affect the coding/decoding and the transmission processes. Good introductions and summaries can help minimize the effects of noise.
» Feedback should always be sought and ample opportunities for clarification be provided to ensure the effectiveness of communication.
» Language registers are something we all have a number of and the proper register should be used for the occasion. Language differences and jargon can impede communication and may serve to alienate recipients.
» Body language provides the most instinctive communication and tends to show true feelings. Those who are in the acting profession have learnt to disguise their own and act out a character's body language – something leaders have to do too. Body language can be both intrinsic and extrinsic, the latter being more easy to control

than the former. Organizations also send out covert communication messages through their organizational body language.

» Surprises to one's subordinates are best avoided when communicating - keep them briefed.

» Audiences differ and so require different means of communication.

» Records of communications should always be kept.

» It is the message that is important, not the technology used to get it across.

» Leaders value the role that networking plays in communication.

Communication is the passing on of information, ideas, feelings, etc. to another party. It may be in the form of words, pictures, music, or gestures but to be effective there must be mutual understanding. More often than not a communication is made up of a complex mixture of the above. Advertisers are extremely proficient at mixing words, pictures and music to build a compelling piece of communication. Each in isolation might have little effect but the synergy they produce in combination can be quite dramatic.

There is a clear structure to the communication process and an understanding of it can help leaders and potential leaders become more effective in their communication. The various parts of the process are covered diagrammatically in Fig. 6.1 below and then in a detailed description. For clarity the coding and decoding processes have been omitted from the feedback loop, but they operate in the reverse order to those on the transmission loop.

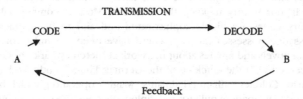

Fig. 6.1 The structure of the communication process represented in four parts.

WHERE COMMUNICATION BEGINS

All communication between humans begins as a thought in somebody's brain. Despite the advances in medicine and biology, we know relatively little about brain processes. We do not even know whether thoughts can be transferred directly despite massive research in this area. Some scientists say that thought transference is a possibility, whilst others discount it and leave it in the realms of science fiction. If it is proved that we can transfer thoughts, then we will have a new means of communication to master - one that might be very difficult indeed as our thoughts are where our ultimate privacy resides.

Tony Buzan, the originator of the technique of mind-mapping, believes that the average human uses a mere 1% of the power of their brain, so it is quite possible that we do have powers that we are as yet unaware of and that the next stage in human evolution may well be mental, rather than physical, as we learn to harness more of our brain potential.[1]

The question is how does a thought, i.e. an electrical/chemical impulse in one brain, end up as an electrical/chemical impulse in another brain with as little change as possible? Given that we cannot read thoughts directly at the moment, the first step involves changing the thought into something more tangible. The process involves coding from the thoughts of the sender and decoding into thoughts in the recipient and an intervening transmission mechanism.

CODING AND DECODING

Codes and cryptography have been used by humans from an early date in our history to keep things secret. Modern commercial and military codes are highly sophisticated and aim to be uncrackable unless one possesses the key. There have been a number of best-selling novels and movies about the work at Bletchley Park, in the UK, concerned with the cracking of the German Enigma code, and about US Army Colonel William Friedman's "Magic" operation, which broke the imperial Japanese military and diplomatic code. This area of human activity is one that seems to fascinate people, as the sales of puzzle books show. However it is something that we all do, subconsciously, every time we communicate.

Every thought that is to be communicated needs to be put into a form that can be transmitted. Humans use a number of such forms, the frequency of use often relating to the degree of importance that a particular sense (i.e. sight, hearing, touch, taste, smell) holds for us in our daily lives. It might be thought that touch, taste, and smell have little place in a discussion about communication in a business series, but every time we put on perfume or aftershave we are sending out a message. A meal as part of a business discussion may be very important. Suffice to say that essence of bread can be put into supermarket air conditioning systems to boost bread sales, and that the aroma of freshly brewed coffee can help to sell houses or so realtors advise. Touch, very important to those with sight defects who use Braille, is also important to us for checking quality and we often make assumptions (sometimes wrong) on the firmness of a handshake. Humans use all their senses to communicate, although vision makes up about 80% of all communications with hearing about 15%.

The vast majority of human communication uses a combination of senses. When we speak (hearing) we often gesticulate (sight); indeed the importance of body language has already been mentioned in this material and will be covered in detail later in this chapter. The same words, e.g. "Can I talk to you?", said with a smile convey a very different message than when said with a scowl. The codes complement one another. However when they do not – as sight is our most heavily used sense – it is the visual message that will be accepted.

The most frequently used code of all is our mother tongue – the language in which we learnt to communicate as children. The same sequence of letters in the same script can be coded differently in different languages. Here are two examples.

» *Fall* means "case" in German and "to go or come down freely" in English.
» *Chef* means both "leader" and "professional cook" in French, but just "professional cook" in English. (Note: the derivation is the same, but the meaning is subject to more permutations in French. A *chef du division* in the European Union hierarchy is a very senior civil servant and not the professional cook for a part of an army, and would be very offended if it was so suggested.)

It is obviously important that all parties who receive a communication are in possession of the same code – something basic, but often forgotten. Decoding is also contextual. We can only transfer into thoughts, and thus into memory, something that we can visualize and if a person has no experience of something, the words and even pictures will be meaningless. This is one reason why the best way to learn a foreign language is to go and live where it is spoken, as then all the clues will be immediately apparent and experienced – the concept behind total immersion language teaching.

It is possible to work with only part of the code. Provided that it supplies the main essentials the brain can often cue in the missing bits although the accuracy is by no means certain. Reading experts believe that we only read a certain percentage of words – we cue in the rest based on experience. This explains why it is difficult to proofread one's own work, as one knows what should be there and the brain subconsciously corrects mistakes. A stranger does not know exactly what should be there and so picks up disparities much more easily. Even if we are stuck, we can sometimes question the other party for clues without revealing that we are unsure of the message. History has a classic example of this from 1942. In May of that year intercepts of communications between units of the Japanese Navy, using a code broken some time earlier by US cryptographers, indicated that a major offensive was being planned against a target referred to as AF in the Japanese code. Where was AF? The US Navy's hunch was that AF was the Midway Islands in the Pacific, but how to be sure? US Navy resources were thin on the ground at the time and the country could not afford to have them in the wrong place. Commander Joseph J. Rochefort USN hit upon a brilliant idea. He had Midway send a message, uncoded to Pearl Harbor, stating that their water distillation plant had broken down. A few days later a Japanese message was intercepted stating that AF had water problems – AF was Midway and the US Navy had time to prepare an ambush. Between June 4 and 6, 1942, the Imperial Japanese Navy lost 4 aircraft carriers, 250 aircraft, and 1 heavy cruiser for the loss of the aircraft carrier USS *Yorktown* – a classic example of using cues and filling in gaps.

Whenever signs are erected it is helpful if organizations use internationally recognized ones to ensure that language is not a problem. There has been considerable progress since the 1950s in ensuring an international standard for road and facility signs that makes it much easier for highway authorities and airports to communicate to users irrespective of the users' language.

TRANSMISSION

Up to the 1840s any message communication that had to go further than a shout, or line of sight, had to be physically transported in the form of writing or a map, or in the memory of a messenger. Today we can communicate at the speed of light (some 186,000 miles per second) – the speed at which electricity or radio waves move. Sound moves much more slowly and its speed depends upon the density of the air. It moves quicker in dense air than thin air, and as sound moves by exciting molecules there is only silence in the vast vacuum of outer space. This is why we see the lightning before we hear the thunder. The two phenomena occur simultaneously but the sound takes longer to travel than the visual image – it is also why one never hears the fatal bullet, as it is travelling supersonically and thus arrives before the sound of the shot.

In the modern world electronic communication allows for pictures, sounds, and words to be sent together, thus greatly aiding the effectiveness of the process. However noise, the subject of the next section, can still be a problem as it can cause corruption to the communication.

NOISE

The reason messages are often misunderstood is that something interferes with the process. Anything that interferes with, or corrupts, communication is called noise. It may be actual physical noise that distorts the message or it may be bad handwriting or conflicting meanings. Noise can also be the use of a dialect that only one of the communicators understands or it could be the differences between an apparently common language (e.g. British English ascribes different words and meanings to certain things than American English). Noise may even be darkness or brightness that hinder the visual process. Anything that distorts the message, prevents reception, or disrupts decoding is noise. In any communication it is important to ensure that noise is kept to a minimum or eliminated altogether. This involves checking that the recipient can actually follow and understand the message – summaries and feedback are very important in minimizing the effects of noise. The use of acronyms and jargon are also examples of noise and will be considered a little later in this chapter. Professions and high-tech suppliers can often be accused of using "in terms" that they understand but others do not, thus creating in-built noise.

Fortunately people can often gain a sense of the meaning of unfamiliar terms and phrases by using the preceding and following phrases to set the term in some form of context. Human nature being what it is, people are often very reluctant to show their ignorance and ask what the term means – hence misunderstandings can and do occur.

TELL THEM, TELL THEM, TELL THEM

It is said that those entering the church as a profession are given a particular piece of advice for the delivery of effective sermons: tell them what you are going to tell them, tell it to them, and then tell them what you have told them. In other words, in the introduction to the topic an indication of content should be given. Then follows the actual content and there is then a summary of the main points. This is a very effective storytelling technique, as it allows the same message to be put forward three times, thus allowing three opportunities for feedback to be given and for clarification to be sought.

Good presenters let their audience know what to expect and then summarize as they go along, as well as at the end, so reinforcing the key messages. If noise affects one telling of the message, it might not affect the others.

LANGUAGE REGISTERS, DIFFERENCES, AND JARGON

We all speak a number of languages, even if we claim not to speak a foreign language. We have one language type (or register) that we use at home, another that we use for work, and yet another that we use with friends. It is important that a communicator can use the language register of the recipient(s) rather than relying on them to learn and understand the language register of the communicator. Plain English, jargon-free terms are the best way to build up a relationship with recipients. Educate them, but only in a manner that is not patronizing or does not make them look or feel foolish.

Governments, both local and national, have gained a reputation for writing documents in a manner that makes them indecipherable to the average person. Organizations such as the Campaign for Plain English in the UK have waged battle on behalf of the man and woman in the street, in order to have official documents in a more readable and understandable style and format.

Even within a single language there are regional and national differences.

» *Vest* in British English means "an undergarment worn under a shirt or blouse." (Americans call this an *undershirt*.)
» *Vest* in American English means "a suit item worn under the jacket." (Britons call this a *waistcoat*.)
» *Suspenders* in British English means "a device used by ladies to hold up stockings." (Americans call these *garters*.)
» *Suspenders* in American English means "a device used by men to hold up trousers." (Britons call these *braces*.)

There is an excellent text by Christopher Davies (who was born in England of a New Zealand father and a Canadian mother, and who currently lives in Florida), entitled *Divided by a Common Language*, which those from one side of the Atlantic visiting and working on the other will find most useful.[2]

Acronyms and jargon are other things to avoid, unless one is very sure that everybody understands them. Using acronyms and jargon can serve to exclude anybody unfamiliar with the terms and can cut the recipient out of the whole communication process, as they might not wish to show their ignorance.

FEEDBACK

The way to ensure that a message has been understood is to request feedback. Just asking "Do you understand?" is a very closed question (i.e. one that can only be answered with a yes/no response) and often receives the answer "Yes", because the recipient believes that they have in fact understood. It is often illuminating to ask "In your own words, what have you been asked to do?" It is often possible to gauge a recipient's understanding by analyzing the subsequent conversation – then it can be judged if both parties are actually on the same wavelength.

History is full of occasions when feedback would have prevented a disaster. The charge of the Light Brigade has already been mentioned in Chapter 1. To it can probably be added Custer's Last Stand, and many cases of poor commercial instructions that yielded what the subordinate thought the manager wanted rather than what the manager intended. The simple task of asking what the recipient understands they have been asked to do, provided that it is done in a non-patronizing manner and without sarcasm, can often show that something the communicator believes to be clear-cut is not so at all.

BODY LANGUAGE AND ACTING

Whatever people may say or write there is one easy way of telling what they are really feeling in a face-to-face situation, and that is through observation of their body language. A person with a red face, gesticulating wildly, is obviously annoyed. But there are more subtle clues that a knowledge of body language can provide, so as to ascertain the true feelings being expressed by a communicator. A person may be saying one thing but their likely behavior will be signaled by their body language. These automatic body responses, which are hard to control unless a person is aware of body language, can be called intrinsic body language clues as they involve the body itself. Extrinsic body language clues involving clothing and so on are considered later in this chapter.

Human beings are unusual for primates in that we are 100% bipeds, i.e. we always walk in an upright position. This confers a major advantage on us as a species, for we can use our very complex arm, hand, and finger joints to manipulate tools whilst still being able to move about. The major disadvantage is that the soft, vulnerable parts of our bodies are exposed to attack. The human skeleton is designed to protect the back – evolutionary history suggests that we once moved on all fours with our fronts close to the ground. Thus, when threatened humans tend to use their arms folded as a defensive shield across the front of the body and this can be very noticeable in body language terms. If somebody claims to be relaxed and they are sitting bolt upright with their arms folded, they are anything but relaxed. They are both defending themselves and poised for either fight or flight. The hormone that controls these particular responses, adrenalin, is often referred to as the fight-or-flight hormone as it puts the body in a state of readiness for action.

A person with their arms away from their body and their palms showing, so a viewer can see that they are not holding a weapon, is displaying the body language of somebody who is being frank, honest, and open. As discussed above, they are not adopting any defensive postures and are displaying an attitude that says "I have nothing to fear from you, so you need fear nothing from me." There will also be good eye contact – another important facet of body language.

Those are just two examples of personal body language. It is difficult to describe subtle facial and bodily movements and so you are advised to look at colleagues and their body language – you will soon be able to feel their mood. Are they fidgeting and therefore nervous about something, can they look you in the eye, are they relaxed? You also need to examine your own body language – what is it saying about you? A basic knowledge of body language is innate. Bullies become more aggressive on seeing a defensive posture; those who value relationships act in the opposite way and try to build up confidence.

Hands can be useful tools for illustrating points, but in most cultures it is considered rude and even threatening to point directly at a person. Personal space should always be maintained. Never get too near to a person, so that they feel that their space is being invaded – you will soon be able to tell, because they will adopt very defensive body language. Equally, never let somebody come so near to you that you feel uncomfortable. Different cultures have different norms on personal space, so it is wise to learn as much as you can.

The skill of an actor or actress is that they can adopt a body language posture that matches the part rather than what they are actually feeling. This is something leaders have to do. Even if they are worried they must give off an air of confidence and authority, so as not to alarm their subordinates.

EXTRINSIC BODY LANGUAGE

The clothes people wear, their jewelry, and even their perfume or aftershave may provide useful clues. A person in business attire will expect to be treated in a business-like manner. Indeed, they may have power-dressed for the occasion. It is also worth remembering that even the very wealthy may dress casually and that many modern fashion trends give little indication of a person's wealth or status. Image is a very important consideration in the way a communication is received and so cannot be ignored.

Objects can sometimes form part of body language. At least one ex-prime minister of the UK, when asked a difficult question, was believed to use the lighting of a pipe to gain time. Keys, pens, and almost anything people hold can be played with – if this happens, the person is displaying nervousness. Beware of such mannerisms, especially if you are delivering a presentation. You might not realize that you are jangling your keys, but your audience will be driven to distraction by it and your message to them will be lost.

In order to study body language, take the time to "people-watch" – a great deal about human behavior can be learnt in this manner.

ORGANIZATIONAL BODY LANGUAGE (OBL)

As part of the work for their book *In Charge of Customer Satisfaction*, Cartwright and Green introduced the term organizational body language (OBL).[3] They had discovered that it was not only individuals who signaled their true feelings through body language, with the resulting dissonance concerning the spoken or written message covered earlier in the chapter. Organizations also exhibited a form of body language that showed their true feelings about the customer. OBL is important to a discussion of communication, as it is the true message that an organization presents to its own employees and the outside world. This is a type of communication that a leader needs to consider very carefully, as the OBL messages should be in line with their vision for the organization.

OBL relates to the whole atmosphere that an organization creates. There are organizations that clearly welcome the customer with open arms and there are those that may claim to but, in fact, send out a message that the customer is actually rather a nuisance who has to be tolerated! It might seem strange that there would be any organization that does not positively welcome its customers, but such organizations do exist – OBL is what customers notice, not the advertisements or mission statements. If the ramps for the physically challenged are around the back of the building, the message is not that ramps are provided (they are now a legal requirement) but that the physically challenged are not welcome in the front door! In case you think that this does not happen, the writer recently visited an organization where the restroom for those in wheelchairs was on the second floor up a narrow flight of stairs – no elevator service was available. Suffice to say it was never used and the explanation for the non-use was that "We never have anybody wanting to use it." That was from an organization that should know better – of course nobody used it, people in wheelchairs take their business elsewhere.

Good leaders will usually pay close attention to this organizational body language concept in addition to personal intrinsic and extrinsic body language.

SURPRISES

A good communicator avoids too many surprises, especially amongst close subordinates. It is important to ensure that those who will have to explain the effects of any communication are well briefed about content before the communication goes out to a more general audience. When communicating with individuals and groups to acquire information, ensure that they are able to assemble any documentation. Let them know in advance what meetings and conversations will be about. It is very easy to play power games and try to catch people out, but much more productive to "catch them in" – it will build up their confidence in themselves and enhance their respect for the leader.

AUDIENCE

Different audiences need different methods to communicate effectively. It is important to ensure that the means matches the audience, rather than the communicator. That said, a sensible person does not try to communicate anything important using a means with which they are uncomfortable. Compromise may be necessary but the audience should come first.

RECORDS

A common fault, even amongst experienced leaders and managers, is to fail to record communications given or received. One never knows when it will be necessary to refer to the content of a communication or even to prove that it took place at a certain time. More and more legal cases require the parties to provide details of communications.

In many jurisdictions it is illegal to record telephone conversations without the consent of the other party and it would be bad manners anyway not to inform somebody that they were being recorded. However, it is not difficult to keep a pad next to the telephone to note conversations. Equally conversations in the office or elsewhere should be noted for future reference.

Just as letters and documents are recorded, so file notes of conversations may be very useful in the future. E-mail is very useful in this respect, as it provides not only a copy but also a receipting mechanism.

IT'S THE MESSAGE, NOT THE TECHNOLOGY

It can be very tempting when delivering a presentation to use every possible item of technology. However, this can be just as distracting to the audience as jangling keys. Good communicators use the most effective technology. Even if a computer projection system is available, don't feel that it has to be used. If a flip chart is at your disposal and you feel more comfortable with it, then use it. Too many pieces of presentational equipment can lead the audience to concentrate on the medium rather than the message.

NETWORKING

There is an old English saying that "it is not what you know, but who you know." Contacts are very important in leadership and are a natural consequence of good communication. Those who aspire to be leaders should take every opportunity to build up their network of contacts. Contacts can be made in both work and social situations and it is important that records are kept. Computer programs to record contacts are freely available and allow for data to be updated and cross-referenced. More than one person has gained a position because their network of contacts was greater than that of other applicants.

KEY LEARNING POINTS
» Communication is made up of the overt spoken or written message and the body language displayed.

» As body language is instinctive, it will be believed over the overt message if there is dissonance between the two.
» Body language can be controlled with training.
» Noise should be minimized wherever possible.
» Feedback is an integral part of the communication process – without it, proper communication has not occurred.
» It is the communicator's responsibility to ensure that the recipients understand the code being used.
» Networking forms an important part of the communication process.
» It is not only the right language that must be employed, but also the correct language register.

NOTES

1 Buzan, A. (1977) *Harnessing the Power of the Parabrain*. Colt, London.
2 Davies, C. (1997) *Divided by a Common Language*. Mayflower Press, Sarasota (FL).
3 Cartright, R. and Green, R. (1997) *In Charge of Customer Satisfaction*. Blackwell, Oxford.

In Practice: Communication Success Stories

» American Express/Ken Chenault.
» The Body Shop/Anita Roddick.
» The Housing Development Finance Corporation (India).

A search for *communication* on the database of Amazon.com, the Internet bookstore, will provide one with over 9000 hits. With this amount of information around, it should be relatively easy to compile three case studies of communication success stories.

However communication is such an everyday part of life that many of the successes are either taken for granted or the actions that promote long-term success occur over a brief period of time. At the beginning of Chapter 2, part of Lincoln's Gettysburg address was quoted. That speech lasted less than two minutes and yet encapsulated nearly a hundred years of history and has affected US development ever since. Vilified as it was by part of the Northern press at the time, the Gettysburg address may well still be quoted in the twenty-second century.

A second problem is that many of the records of communication concern failures not successes. It is often said that human beings learn more from their failures than they ever do from their successes, hence making it more useful to examine why something went wrong – which may be only 1% of the time – than why nothing went wrong, or "nothing out of the ordinary happened," which is the other 99% of the time.

L.T.C. Rolt's first edition of his book *Red for Danger* on British railway accidents covered 68 major train wrecks in detail.[1] Of these at least 50 were not technical failures or related to snow, rain, etc. – they were failures in the ability of human beings to communicate effectively and in about 40 of the cases a simple feedback loop would have prevented death and disaster striking out of the blue. Railways have been very important to communication, not only for physical transportation but also for the increase in speed of travel that they brought, which meant that communications needed to be faster and more accurate than ever. When two people are walking towards each other at 5mph there is plenty of time to take avoiding action. When two trains moving at over 50mph and weighing several tons are sharing the same piece of track, effective communication becomes very much a matter of life or death.

If a life had not been lost and five other people seriously injured, one could be amused by what happened at Menheniot in the county of Cornwall, UK, in December 1873. Even at this late stage in the UK's railway development, this remote station on a single-track line lacked signals – all instructions were verbal. The station itself consisted of the main line and a loop. Both tracks were occupied by freight trains, with another train approaching from the west and due to enter the station after the eastbound train had departed. The person in charge at Menheniot was aware that the train from the west was due and so shouted to the conductor of the stationary eastbound train (whom he knew), "Right away Dick." To his horror both the trains in the station started to move. He was unaware that the conductor of the other train was also called Dick. That failure to use a suitable procedure cost a life.

The reason that so many transportation and military failures in communication are recorded is that they have been the subject of official inquiries for longer than other human activities. Thus records of failure exist, although there are no records of all the millions of times the system worked perfectly.

In choosing the cases for this chapter, the aim has been to illustrate an organizational commitment to communication, a personal commitment to communication, and the relationship between communicator and recipient. American Express, The Body Shop, and the Housing Development Finance Corporation in India are very different organizations with one thing in common – a commitment to excellent communication for the benefit of all their stakeholders.

CASE STUDY 1: AMERICAN EXPRESS/KEN CHENAULT

American Express has become one of those organizations that has a global presence and is used by those who are not necessarily from the US, despite the word American in its title. As one of the first charge card providers to enter a global market, the Amex brand has become synonymous with travel services. Despite the use of charge cards on a national or even global basis being a recent commercial development, made possible by the synergy of computer and telephone technology, the origins of American Express are to be found as early as 1850. American Express, like Thomas Cook in the UK, grew up as a direct result of the increase in travel brought about by railway development. American Express is now the largest travel agency in the world.

Headquartered in New York, Amex, in spite of its highly American title, is listed not only on the New York Stock Exchange but also on the London and Paris exchanges. Amex has grown as global travel has

increased, and by 2000 was providing a very solid financial performance. Net revenues for 2000, the 150th anniversary of the company,
were $22,085mn earned by the global workforce of 88,850. Other
financial strong points of 2000 were as follows.

» Financial performance met or exceeded Amex's long-term targets of
   12–15% growth in earnings per share, return on equity of 18–20%,
   and revenue growth of at least 8%, on average and over time.
» Amex passed the 50 million mark in terms of the number of its cards
   in use worldwide, thus increasing its market share in the US and in
   many of the most important international markets.
» Lending approached $32bn at the year end 2000, up 24% from
   1999, and exceeded the year 2000 goal of $30bn set in 1995 – a
   target which, when set, was considered to be more aspirational than
   achievable.
» American Express Financial Advisors (AEFA) reported earnings
   growth across most business lines for the year, with increases in
   overall asset levels, sales, and the number of advisors.
» Earnings also rose at American Express Bank (AEB), gaining momen-
   tum by shifting the focus of the business from corporate clients to
   individuals and financial institutions.
» Amex implemented a new structure to help grow the business on a
   global basis.

The challenge for Amex post-2000 is to reduce expenses, as these
have been growing at the same rate as revenues, and deal with the
uncertainty of global market conditions.

Ken Chenault must take much of the credit for the continuing success
of Amex. His very appointment was an organizational body language
message to corporate America (see Chapter 6 for a fuller discussion of
organizational body language). When he was first appointed president
and COO (chief operating officer) of Amex in 1997, the then CEO,
Harvey Golub, announced that Chenault was to be his chosen successor
upon his retirement in 2001. In a profile of Chenault, Marquardt and
Berger quote *Business Week* which described him as possessing all-
round leadership capabilities.[2] Chenault became the highest-ranking
African-American in US business. That was an important message that
Amex sent to the US and the world, whether intentionally or not. It

was a message that was reinforced when President George W. Bush appointed another high-profile African-American, General Colin Powell (leader of the allied forces in Operation Desert Storm in the early 1990s), as his secretary of state and thus the public face of US diplomacy.

Much has been written about the barriers to both ethnic minorities and women gaining positions within the executive function of organizations. That the glass ceiling, which divides those who do get to the top from those who don't, exists is unfortunately a fact well profiled by authorities such as Davidson and Bahl,[3] Davidson and Cooper.[4] Stith,[5] and Wirth.[6] The breaking of this ceiling by people like Ken Chenault, Colin Powell, and Anita Roddick (the subject of the next case study) is a communication far stronger than mere words, as it provides an example that all can follow.

Chenault joined American Express in 1981 at the age of 29 and rose rapidly through the organization, whilst building up an impressive network of contacts. By 2000 he was not only employed by American Express, but also served on the boards of IBM, Quaker Oats, and the Brooklyn Gas Company in the commercial sector and those of the National Collegiate Athletic Association, the NYU Medical Center, the National Center on Addiction and Substance Abuse, and the Arthur Ashe Institute for Urban Health (named after the famous African-American tennis star). Chenault also has membership of the Council on Foreign Relations and the Dean's Advisory Board of Harvard Law School. These have been listed in full to show how his contacts are not just commercial but philanthropic, medical, governmental, and legal – just the type of network a leader needs. He is also very active in the community, again adding to his list of contacts. However Chenault appears to want the community involvement, rather than an opportunity to network, and thus comes over as honest – which he appears to be.

Chenault's communication skills have allowed him to ensure that his vision for American Express reaches all employees and important decision-makers outside the organization. He is very much described as a team player and, whilst he is clearly in charge, it appears that he is also respected for who he is. When Amex was threatened by a boycott in Boston in 1991, Chenault as head of the relevant Amex division at the time was the one who went out and met with those who were protesting (not radicals but a group of restaurant owners concerned at Amex fees). His communication skills as a speaker, and also as a listener, are credited with resolving the problem with the minimum of adverse publicity.

Chenault leads by ensuring that people know what is happening – this is as much a communication skill as a leadership one. As this material has tried to demonstrate, communication and leadership are not different business attributes – they are one and the same.

Chenault has been the subject of countless articles both in business journals and magazines dedicated to African-Americans. Examples of these are included in Chapter 9. Chenault's rapid rise through the ranks at American Express is represented in Fig. 7.1 below.

KEY INSIGHTS

» The importance of a comprehensive network of contacts cannot be underestimated.
» As shown during the Boston boycott, a leader may need to deploy their communication skills on the front line.
» Integrity impresses people and aids credibility - a communicator with no credibility is not a communicator.
» Vision is one of the most important things that is ever communicated.
» The glass ceiling is becoming rightly fragile - Chenault was able to break through it, in part, because of his excellent communication skills and well-developed network.

CASE STUDY 2: THE BODY SHOP/ANITA RODDICK

"Leadership is fundamentally about communication and dialogue..."

Anita Roddick, 2000

Since its inception in 1976, The Body Shop has pioneered socially responsive business practices and challenged the nature of the cosmetics industry. Success has transformed it into a global household name

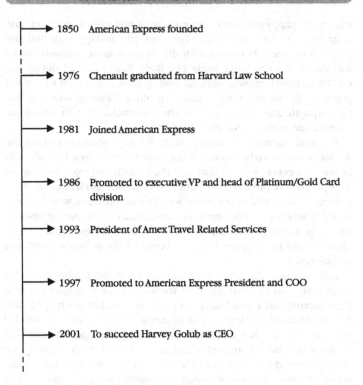

1850   American Express founded

1976   Chenault graduated from Harvard Law School

1981   Joined American Express

1986   Promoted to executive VP and head of Platinum/Gold Card
        division

1993   President of Amex Travel Related Services

1997   Promoted to American Express President and COO

2001   To succeed Harvey Golub as CEO

Fig. 7.1   A timeline charting Ken Chenault's successful career at American
Express.

and by 1987 Anita Roddick had accepted the Confederation of British
Industry's award for Company of the Year. Unfortunately for Roddick
this was the time that business appeared to have reached its peak.
In her autobiography, *Business as Unusual*, she gives the impression
that throughout the 1990s just about everything that could go wrong
did.[7] Organizationally, the enterprise had spiraled into a complex and
inefficient mess, described in her own words as "a Lego set from
Hell." The financial bottom line was under pressure from competitors

who were happy to mimic the packaging and ethical stand of The Body Shop, without the effort that goes into making sure that the organization really is trading ethically. Perhaps most damaging of all was the spate of negative press The Body Shop received during the mid-1990s from commentators queuing up to question their values and practices. By the end of the century, lay-offs and change were high on the corporate agenda as The Body Shop restructured in an attempt to reinvent the brand for the new millennium.

As David Korten has pointed out in *When Corporations Rule the World*, business is where much of the modern power base lies, whereas in previous eras it was the State and the Church that exercised power over people's day-to-day lives.[8] In terms of power and influence, there is no more powerful institution in society than business, which is why Roddick believes it is now more important than ever before for business to assume a moral leadership. Her creed is that business should not be about money but responsibility. It should be about public good, not private greed.

Roddick, born in 1942, grew up with her three siblings in the seaside town of Littlehampton, on the south coast of England, where their parents had a small café/diner. It was from her mother that she first learnt about the importance of caring for the customer. Trained as a teacher, Roddick and her husband, Gordon, opened their first business venture, a hotel and restaurant, in 1971. However, even then she was considering the idea of a new way of promoting and selling cosmetics based on ethical principles. Roddick has no problems with wealth; she is a wealthy woman in her own right but is concerned that greed has now become culturally acceptable.

Her Body Shop concept of providing cosmetics that were made from natural products, not tested on animals, and retailed in such a manner that maximum use was made of recycling, refilling, and reusing began in 1976 in the old seaside resort of Brighton, UK, and swiftly grabbed the public imagination. The idea of an ethical organization fitted the mood of the times and The Body Shop soon began to expand.

By 1988 the organization had expanded into the US and in 1990 franchising operations began, such had been the growth of the concept. The growth was also assisted by Roddick's decision to source materials from local communities in the developing world rather than large suppliers. Meeting these groups gave her an opportunity to set up lines of communication to them and for The Body Shop to help communities grow and develop skills and confidence. Moving into the US showed Roddick how much further advanced US women were in networking skills as compared to their colleagues in the UK. Roddick sees networking as a key business skill and hopes that British women will attain the degree of networking competence seen in the US.

Communication has been a key concern of Roddick's as these statements from her autobiography indicate.

"Communication is the key for any global business."

"As a business you have to listen to your customers at exactly the same time as telling them where you're coming from."

"I used to wish that by the Millennium we wouldn't be a cosmetics company with a communications arm, we would be a communications company with a cosmetic arm. We are not there yet."

"Leadership is fundamentally about communication and dialogue."

"Nothing can substitute for a live leader listening and responding."

"Every entrepreneur is a great storyteller."[9]

Roddick has championed the concept of leadership by storytelling, as introduced in the early chapters of this material. She gives storytelling the priority she does because of its ability to fire the imagination and that is what she looks for in her people. Roddick states how effective leadership for her staff involves shared vision, words, symbols, and body language. It may seem strange to read about the importance of giving staff a hug but Roddick is unafraid to say that this may be part of a leader's role in the appropriate circumstances.

The Body Shop suffered a downturn in turnover and profits towards the end of the 1990s and this presented Roddick with a new challenge – how to communicate lay-offs to a workforce that had been extremely loyal. Staff were kept informed and, hard though the decisions were, The Body Shop restructured with the loss of three hundred posts. It was a traumatic time for Roddick, but leaders must take the rough with the smooth. As communication skills are greatly valued and developed at The Body Shop, many of those leaving were well equipped to either gain new positions elsewhere or to start up on their own. The organization has not neglected its communications with the outside world. The Body Shop Foundation acts as a vehicle for donations (£3.5mn to 180 groups worldwide in the first six years since its inception in 1990), and Roddick and her senior team work with suppliers in the field and with the all-important franchise partners.

It was announced in 2001 that Roddick was considering a £290mn ($403mn) deal to sell The Body Shop to a Mexican nutritional supplements group. Shares in The Body Shop jumped almost 16% on this news, as the company confirmed it had received a bid approach. Roddick and her husband, who co-founded and who jointly chair The Body Shop group, believe that Grupo Omnilife share their ethical approach to business. Omnilife, founded by Jorge Vergara Madrigal, a 45-year-old self-made billionaire, has been built around providing vitamin and mineral supplements for the poor of Mexico. The talks, which were still at an early stage at the time of writing, started when Omnilife approached Roddick informally. The Roddicks hold just under 25% of The Body Shop.

In 1997 Roddick had previously tried to make the group private with the aim of turning it into a charity, but this proposal proved to be financially non-viable. Shares in the group have languished somewhat since 1996 – remaining stubbornly far from their highest level of £3.70 reached at the start of 1992 – so it may be that investors will see the Mexican approach as a way of moving the organization forward financially.

Ethical policies

The Websites for The Body Shop (UK, US, Canada, Denmark, Germany, Australia, Japan, and Korea) contain information and communications about products, as do most Websites, but also lay out the ethical policies of the organization in some detail. Whilst this can lead to challenges if parts of the media discover that a policy is not being followed, it allows customers and staff to see exactly what The Body Shop stands for. Roddick also speaks at many conferences and seminars, and made her commitment to fair trade quite explicit by writing the foreword to David Ransom's book on the subject.[10]

The Body Shop philosophy can be found in full on their Website, but a synopsis is provided below:

» mutually beneficial trading relationships with suppliers, franchisees, and customers, based on trust and respect but maintaining commercial viability;
» respect for human and civil rights, as set out in the Universal Declaration of Human Rights, throughout business activity – this includes workers' rights to a safe, healthy working environment; fair wages; no discrimination on the basis of race, creed, gender, or sexual orientation; and no physical coercion of any kind;
» support for long-term, sustainable relationships with communities in need, with special attention to those minority groups, women, and disadvantaged peoples who are socially and economically marginalized;
» use of environmentally sustainable resources wherever technically and economically viable;
» purchasing based on a system of screening and investigation of the ecological credentials of finished products, ingredients, packaging, and suppliers;
» promotion of animal protection throughout business activity;
» opposition to use of animals for testing in the cosmetics and toiletries industry;
» no testing of ingredients or products on animals, nor the commissioning of others to do so on The Body Shop's behalf; and
» use of The Body Shop's purchasing power to stop suppliers using animals for testing.

Coming from a major global company these are astonishing concepts, given that nearly every other organization talks about being a market leader, financially sound, etc. As will be seen in Fig. 7.2 below, Roddick has never been afraid to add her name and that of the organization to causes she believes in. Whilst this can cause problems with governments, especially as she is outspoken about human rights, this has not deterred Roddick or her husband. Cynics might say that "all publicity is good publicity" but there is no evidence that Roddick takes up

1942 Roddick born in UK

1971 First business venture with husband Gordon – hotel and restaurant

1976 First branch of The Body Shop in Brighton, UK

1978 First international Body Shop, a kiosk in Brussels

1976 First campaign – Save the Whales, with Greenpeace. The Body Shop Charter prepared by staff

1988 Body Shop enter US market

1990 Romanian Relief Drive begun to renovate orphanages in post-Communist Romania. The Body Shop Foundation founded. Child Development Center opened at Head Office, first purpose-built UK company day care center

1991 After three years of producing soap for The Body Shop, Soapworks opened a children's playground in Easterhouse, Glasgow, Scotland. *The Big Issue* magazine sold by homeless people launched in London and supported by The Body Shop. Joint letter writing campaign by Amnesty International and The Body Shop instrumental in freeing several prisoners of conscience. *Body and Soul*, Anita Roddick's first autobiography, published

Fig. 7.2 A timeline mapping the ambitious ethical trading of The Body Shop over 25 years.

1992   Brazilian Healthcare Project established through The Body Shop

Foundation in conjunction with Brazilian agencies; funding and

organizing immunization procedures, medical checks, hospital

renovation, construction and health education for over 4,000

Indians in 18 Amazon villages

Community store opened in Harlem, New York

US Voter Registration drive signed up 40,000 more people to vote

in US Presidential Elections

1993   A Community Trade supplier in India established. US turnover now

$44.6 million – profits $1.9 million

1994   Paternity leave offered to all male Company employees, well in

advance of UK government and EU plans. Children's school

opened by Community Trade supplier in India. Major award to

The Body Shop Canada for Domestic Violence campaign.

Link with the Missing Persons Helpline, converting Body Shop

trucks into moving billboards

1995   Visit funded and organized by the Body Shop Supply Company

from Byelorussian children with 'Children Of Chernobyl' charity.

Petition of 1.5 million signatures in support of women's rights

presented by Body Shop delegates at 4th World Conference on Women in

Beijing, China. The Body Shop starts its Internet Website

Fig. 7.2   (*Continued*).

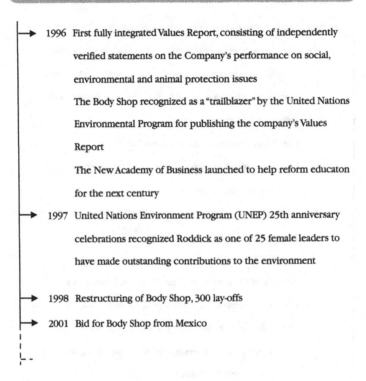

1996 First fully integrated Values Report, consisting of independently
verified statements on the Company's performance on social,
environmental and animal protection issues
The Body Shop recognized as a "trailblazer" by the United Nations
Environmental Program for publishing the company's Values
Report
The New Academy of Business launched to help reform educaton
for the next century

1997 United Nations Environment Program (UNEP) 25th anniversary
celebrations recognized Roddick as one of 25 female leaders to
have made outstanding contributions to the environment

1998 Restructuring of Body Shop, 300 lay-offs

2001 Bid for Body Shop from Mexico

Fig. 7.2 *(Continued).*

campaigns for commercial reasons. It appears that she acts out her
ethical beliefs in business life.

More and more investors are demanding ethical portfolios, and in a
1999 survey over 40% of the 22,000 consumers questioned worldwide
claimed to have boycotted a product in response to concerns either
about the manufacturer, retailer, or country of origin. Naomi Klein in
her book, *No Logo*, has shown how public opinion on cheap and child
labor in certain parts of the world in the US affected Nike when a
boycott was threatened.[11] The consumer is beginning to wield power
not just on price and quality but also on ethics.

One can only advise anybody concerned about the way they communicate to read *Business as Unusual*, as Roddick exemplifies the communication skills of a good leader – one who listens, responds, and understands the totality of a message, composed as most are of more than just words.

KEY INSIGHTS

» Communicating a vision lets everybody know what you stand for.
» Storytelling has a place in the world of business.
» Communication and leadership skills go hand in hand.
» Leaders need to listen and respond.
» Networking skills are vital in leadership and business.

CASE 3: THE HOUSING DEVELOPMENT FINANCE CORPORATION (INDIA)

Incorporated in 1977 with a share capital of 100 million rupees, the Housing Development Finance Corporation (HDFC) is now the largest residential mortgage finance institution in the country. The corporation has had a series of share issues raising its capital to 1190 million rupees. By the end of the financial year 1999-2000 the net worth of the corporation was 20,960 million rupees ($439,652mn).

The core business of HDFC is to provide financial assistance to help Indians enjoy home ownership. As HDFC state, the road to success is a tough and challenging journey in the dark where only obstacles light the path. However, success on a terrain like this is not without a solution. To those used to Western prose this may sound rather flowery, but in Asia business, spirituality, and life itself are not as clearly delineated as in the West, as the writer himself found when working in India during 1993-5.

HDFC have a philosophy, well known in the West and the Asia-Pacific region, of total customer satisfaction. The company has shown the courage to innovate, the skill to understand the customer, and the desire to give them the best. By 2001, over one million customers had used

HDFC's services. The HDFC objective, from the beginning, has been to enhance residential housing stock, promote home ownership, and offer products including home loans, deposit schemes, and property-related services. Also offered are specialized financial services to the customer base through partnerships with some of the best financial institutions worldwide. Foreclosure is frowned upon in India and thus the relationship with the customer must rely on trust, rather than fear, as is the case in some mortgage markets.

For those in the West and the UK in particular, with its long tradition of home ownership, HDFC may sound like many of the traditional building societies or savings and loan operations seen in every town and city. However India has not had the same tradition of home ownership that the US and the UK have developed. In particular the concept of a mortgage provider dealing directly with the customer was not widespread in the 1970s.

The sheer size of the population means that housing is always going to be a major issue. India ranks second only to China among the world's most populous countries, with a population by 2001 of well over one billion with an annual increase of about 230 million. The overall population density is about 300 persons per sq. km (about 712 per sq. mile). More than 70% of India's population lives in rural areas. With a growing middle class the economic prosperity of India is rising all the time, although there are still areas of intense poverty. Education is highly valued and literacy rates are ever increasing. India, the largest democracy in the world, is a major industrial power having its own satellite capability and a military nuclear program.

A rising middle class, many of whom are well traveled and have relatives in other parts of the world, has led to a need for increased levels of customer care. Indian customers have been given more and more choice in the past few years as foreign companies have begun manufacturing in India – currency restrictions on the rupee have eased the transaction of foreign purchases.

HDFC was one of the early exponents of high-quality customer care in the Indian market and soon discovered that this meant considering the way the communication process worked and the importance of organizational body language. As Deepak S. Parekh has made clear, when a customer enters HDFC's premises for the first time they will come with a certain set of expectations. However because of the high-quality service they receive, the next visit will have enhanced expectations and HDFC must then meet these. His aim has been that in all business, including its manner of communication, HDFC will be a business with a human face – this of course means that aspects such as organizational body language have to be considered, just as human body language cannot be ignored.

Feedback systems

A large number of Indian organizations have embarked upon major training programs for individuals or groups of staff in the past decade. Hindustan Motor Company, United Brewers, Kerala Bank, and HDFC are all examples. The aim has been to hone management and communication skills amongst the staff in order to be competitive in a more global market. Increasingly the financial services market is global and indigenous organizations cannot depend upon local loyalty without high standards of service delivery. Staff training and the development of an in-house feedback system have been priorities for HDFC, as has the introduction of inter-branch teams to improve the communication between various parts of the organization. As organizations grow the need for consistency can sometimes be lost, and the improvement of internal communications between teams rather than a journey through the hierarchy is an excellent means of addressing this problem.

Parekh has been awarded honors for both himself and HDFC. It is not a large organization, as the major global financial players are, but recognizes the vital role of communication, feedback, and knowing the customer in an economy with a great deal of potential. The company's progress onwards and upwards is shown in Fig. 7.3 below.

KEY INSIGHTS

» A commitment to quality is always a positive communication to the customer.
» Feedback is important and formal systems should be put in place.

1977 HDFC founded

1993 HDFC profiled in Indian press and lauded for its commitment to service

1998 Parekh awarded Qimpro Platinum Service award

2001 1 millionth customer and 85 locations

Fig. 7.3 A timeline depicting the steady rise of the HDFC.

- Inter-branch communication should be encouraged to aid standards and consistency.
- The vision of the chair permeates the whole organization through active communication.

NOTES

1 Rolt, L.T.C. (1955) *Red for Danger*. Bodley Head, London.
2 Marquardt, M.J. and Berger, N.O. (2000) *Global Leaders for the 21st Century*. State University of New York Press, Albany.
3 Davidson, M. and Bahl, K. (1997) *The Black and Ethnic Minority Woman Manager*. Paul Chapman, London.
4 Davidson, M. and Cooper, G. (1992) *Shattering the Glass Ceiling*. Paul Chapman, London.
5 Stith, A. (1998) *Breaking the Glass Ceiling: Sexism and racism in corporate America*. Bryant & Dillon, Orange (NJ).

6 Wirth, L. (2000) *Breaking through the Glass Ceiling*. International Labor Organization, Geneva.

7 Roddick, A. (2000) *Business as Unusual*. HarperCollins, London.

8 Korten, D. (1995) *When Corporations Rule the World*. Earthscan, London.

9 Roddick, *Business...*, op. cit.

10 Ransom, D. (2001) *The No-Nonsense Guide to Fair Trade*. New Internationalist, Oxford.

11 Klein, N. (2000) *No Logo: No space, no choice, no jobs, taking aim at the brand bullies*. Flamingo, London.

Key Communication Concepts and Thinkers

» Glossary and key concepts in communication.
» Key thinkers on business communication.

A GLOSSARY OF COMMUNICATION

Allegory – a message, story, play, poem, or even a picture or movie in which the meaning is represented symbolically.

Body language – the messages displayed through the posture or appearance of a person.

Branding – originally used as a term to indicate the addition of a mark to a possession (especially livestock) as a sign of ownership. Branding is now used as a term to describe the attachment of a name or logo to a product as a means of adding value. Brands acquire their own values of quality, reliability, style, etc. and this is what adds value over an identical but non-branded product.

Coding – the process whereby thoughts are put into a form that can be transmitted to another. The code is normally in the form of words, symbols, music, gestures, etc. The sender of the communication needs to ensure that the intended recipient knows which code is being used and also possesses a copy of that code.

Culture – the values, attitudes, and beliefs ascribed to and accepted by a group, nation, or organization. In effect, ''the way we do things around here.''

Cuneiform – wedge-shaped writing impressed into clay as used by the ancient Sumerians and Babylonians.

Decoding – the process whereby a transmitted communication is reconfigured into a thought pattern by the recipient of the communication. Decoding can only occur if the recipient is privy to the code being used by the sender. Humans keep most of the coding information in their memories but also have a set of codebooks available – language and subject dictionaries.

Dissonance – a psychological conflict caused by receiving two opposing ideas of which one will represent reality and the other falsity. Humans will normally resolve any conflict between an overt message and body language by believing the latter.

Extrinsic body language – body language related to clothing, perfume, etc., which are within the control of the individual.

Feedback – the process of checking to see whether a communication has been properly received and correctly understood. Feedback turns communication from a linear into a circular process.

Information and communication technology (ICT) - technology related to the connection of computer and communication technology to produce a synergy between them. ICT was originally known as IT (information technology). However more and more computer-type applications also involve communication with other computers or communication devices, hence the adoption of the abbreviation ICT.

Intrinsic body language - body language related to the physical body, which is controlled through the nervous or hormone systems. It is thus hard to control.

Logo - a symbol adopted by an organization to represent the organization graphically. Logos not only come to represent the name of the organization or brand, but also the values associated with it. Logos are so important as a recognition feature that they are heavily protected against copying or counterfeiting.

Networking - the building-up of a network of contacts. The network acts in a synergic manner. Work and social occasions provide opportunities for networking.

Non-verbal communication - communication other than by speech or writing, applied especially to body language.

Organizational body language (OBL) - the messages that an organization sends out through the way its premises, signs, etc. are arranged.

Synergy - a phenomenon where the sum of the parts is greater than the whole. A computer and a camera connected to a telephone can aid communication far more than might be expected by an examination of the individual capabilities of the three components.

Transmission - the physical movement of a communication from the sender to the recipient.

Verbal communication - communication in speech or writing.

KEY THINKERS

Cairncross, Frances

In considering what will be the most significant economic factor to shape the world's future, Frances Cairncross, senior editor at *The Economist*, believes that it's the "death of distance" caused by the communications revolution. Her work suggests that the relationships between people will change radically within the twenty-first century, affecting both people's home and work lives, and the way government operates. Because the Internet removes all geographic boundaries, Cairncross asserts that people and businesses will relocate wherever they want, making it difficult for countries to enforce tax laws. Governments will be under extreme pressure to offer the best public services to attract businesses and individuals. Cairncross also predicts that people's reading and writing skills will improve because they'll have to communicate effectively using electronic means. Although Cairncross voices concern over an inability to "control" what goes over the Internet, she ultimately looks on the communications revolution as enabling a more liberal exchange of ideas.

From the advent of electronic communications, there's been talk about how the world has been shrinking. Cairncross argues the future from an economist's standpoint rather than that of a communication expert, and thus she brings together two disciplines. The growing ease and speed of communication is creating a world where distance has little to do with our ability to work or interact together. Cairncross predicts that it won't be long before people organize globally on the basis of language and three basic time shifts – one for the Americas, one for Europe, and one for east Asia and Australia. Much of the work done on a computer can be done from anywhere. Workers can code software in one part of the world and pass it to a company hundreds of miles away that will assemble the code for marketing. Many airline tickets are now processed in India, the details having been downloaded from New York, London, Paris, etc. The consequence of workers able to earn a living from anywhere is, she argues, that countries may find themselves competing for citizens as people relocate for reasons ranging from lower taxes to nicer weather.

Cairncross has written a large number of volumes on economics and only the most important for communication studies are listed below.

Highlights

Books:

» (1997) *The Death of Distance: How the communications revolution will change our lives*. Orion Business, London.

» (2001) *The Death of Distance 2.0: How the communications revolution will change our lives*. Texere, London.

Klein, Naomi

A Canadian, Naomi Klein is a journalist and commentator who has been especially concerned with the effects of branding and logos on society. In her book *No Logo* (shortlisted for the Guardian First Book Award in 2000), she explores the effects that logos have on the relationship between company and customer, and delves into the issues of outsourcing that leave a company with just a logo and a marketing operation as goods are made to contract. She also examines the power of the consumer to make large organizations accountable. Whilst mainly considering US-based multinationals, she analyzes the behavior of Shell and other European operations too. *No Logo* contains a useful reading list for those interested in studying the effect of branding and logos on corporate communications.

Highlights

Books:

» (2000) *No Logo: No space, no choice, no jobs, taking aim at the brand bullies*. Flamingo, London.

Lewis, Richard

Richard D. Lewis is an authority on the management of cultural difference. He is the founder of the magazine *Cross Culture*, of considerable interest to those involved in global expansion, and in addition to speaking over 12 languages he has worked with a large number of major multinational organizations. Lewis makes the point that mutual understanding and sensitivity lie at the heart of managing across cultures. In both *When Cultures Collide* (2000) and *Cross-Cultural Communication* (1999), Lewis stresses the importance of ensuring that the communications process is as robust as possible. The same words and phrases can mean different things in different cultures and this is an important point to consider when a global organization is issuing policy documents and so on.

Having developed a model for cultural analysis, Lewis has produced two PC-based packages. The first, the Cross-Cultural Assessor, is a tool for cross-cultural analysis applicable to both individuals and across an organization. The Cross-Cultural Assessor is a multimedia product designed to assist individuals and organizations in measuring, building, and managing cross-cultural skills and characteristics. The second package, Gulliver, provides both cross-cultural training and a database to set up "what if" scenarios. Gulliver is a computer-based training product – delivered either online or via CD-ROM – and is a joint venture between Richard Lewis and Price Waterhouse Coopers. The purpose of Gulliver is to help people involved in international business to perform successfully across cultures.

Highlights

Books:

» (1999) *Cross-Cultural Communication: A visual approach*. Transcreen, London.
» (2000) *When Cultures Collide*. Nicholas Brealey, London.

Journals:

» (10 issues p.a.; subscription only) *Cross Cultural Letter to International Managers*. Richard Lewis Communications, UK and worldwide.

McQuail, Denis

A graduate of history and social studies at Oxford, McQuail worked initially at the University of Leeds in northern England at the newly founded (1959) Centre for Television Research. He assisted the first head of the Centre, Dr J. Trenaman, and was a colleague of his successor, Dr J. Blumler. During the 1960s, he collaborated in a number of research projects concerned with the influence of television in politics, education, social values, and cultural taste. Best known from this period are his various works on the influence of television and the political process. British television was beginning to cover both politics and the election process in much greater detail in the 1960s than ever before, hence a considerable interest in the influence of the medium was developing. McQuail continued this interest in political communication in different ways, for instance in research into young voters in Britain during the 1970s and into the European elections beginning in 1979.

In 1965 he moved to the University of Southampton, where he started to lecture in sociology, with particular reference to mass communication and public opinion. One result of this was the publication *Towards a Sociology of Mass Communications* (1969). His research in this period was mainly directed towards studies of the audience, with particular reference to the origin and nature of motives leading to media use and the shaping of response to media.

Since the 1960s, Denis McQuail has developed further interests in communication theory, leading to various analytic and synthesizing works including three editions of a book entitled *Mass Communication Theory* (1983; 1987; 1994). This represents an attempt to relate theory of media with theory of society, and also to contribute to the development of a more coherent body of theory for the new subject of "communication science." This work was stimulated by a year spent as visiting professor at the Annenberg School of Communication at the University of Pennsylvania. During the fall semester of 1974 he was acting associate professor of communication research at Tampere University in Finland. In Tampere he completed another widely distributed text, *Communication* (1975).

In the mid-1970s, he worked as an academic consultant for the Royal Commission on the Press (1974–7), with particular responsibility for a broad evaluative study of the content of British newspapers. This research has since stimulated a continued interest in questions of media policy and performance, especially in the wider European context. In 1977, he was appointed to the chair of mass communication at the University of Amsterdam, where he has remained since. He has collaborated in research into the diversity of media in the Netherlands and also joined two cross-European comparative research groups, one concerned with the role of television in the campaigns for elections to the European parliament, another (the Euro Media Research Group) which has been studying the relations between electronic media change and public policy in Western Europe since 1982.

Denis McQuail was one of the three founding editors of the *European Journal of Communication* (see Chapter 9) and continues to edit the journal. He has held a number of visiting positions in different countries.

He was appointed as one of the first holders of the UNESCO chair in mass communication at the University of Moscow, where he lectured in 1994. He has also lectured at the John F. Kennedy School of Government, at Harvard, and the Seijo University in Japan.

His theoretical and empirical research interests have tended to converge on the territory where changes in media systems (the consequence of technology, politics, and social change) interact with public policies for media. Denis McQuail has recently spent much time in studying the question of public interest in the standards of media performance. The publication of *Media Performance: Mass communication in the public interest* (1992) is the result of this work. It was helped by the opportunity to spend a semester at the Gannett Center for Media Research at Columbia University in New York.

Highlights

Books:

- » (1969) *Towards a Sociology of Mass Communications*. Macmillan, London.
- » (1972) (ed.) *Sociology of Mass Communications: Selected readings*. Penguin, Harmondsworth.
- » (1984) *Communication*, 2nd ed. Longman, London.
- » (1992) *Media Performance: Mass communication in the public interest*. Sage, London.
- » (1993) (with S. Windahl) *Communication Models for the Study of Mass Communications*, 2nd ed. Longman, London.
- » (1994) *Mass Communication Theory: An introduction*, 3rd ed. Sage, London.

Articles, papers, and studies:

- » (1977) *Analysis of Newspaper Content*, Royal Commission on the Press, Research Series 4. HMSO, London.
- » (1979) The historicity of a science of mass media: time, place, circumstances and the effects of mass communication. Inaugural speech, University of Amsterdam.
- » (1986) "Is media theory adequate to the challenge of the new communication technologies?" in M. Ferguson (ed.), *New Communication*

Technologies and the Public Interest, pp. 1–17. Sage, Beverly Hills and London.

» (1987) "The functions of communication: a non-functionalist overview, in C.R. Berger and S.H. Chaffee (eds), *Handbook of Communication Science*, pp. 327–49. Sage, Beverly Hills and London.

Shea, Michael

Visiting professor of personal and corporate communications at the Graduate Business School, University of Strathclyde, and the Scottish member of the Independent Television Commission, Shea is a former diplomat who for ten years was press secretary to the Queen and later was head of public affairs at Hanson Plc. He is currently a non-executive director of a number of other companies and is author of some twenty books on fiction and non-fiction.

His work on communications has been in the field of personal impact and he has brought his considerable experience to bear on advising on how best to present oneself. As a mover in the highest circles he provides valuable advice about such matters as body language. It is acknowledged that the possession of good communication skills is one of the keys to personal and business success today. Our reputations, jobs, and promotions have become dependent upon the way we present ourselves to others and the way we communicate with both individuals and groups. Evidence exists to suggest that it is in the first 15 seconds that our reputations and images are formed by others. This psychological first impression – "the primacy effect" – is often the key to success in a presentation, interview, or negotiation meeting. Shea shows how to prepare for and execute that vital first 15 seconds in any communication situation. He also examines other areas of communication, including how to inspire an audience; non-verbal communication; dress and body language; avoiding interview pitfalls; public speaking; business presentations; influence and persuasion. In doing so, he presents some of the tricks used by lawyers, preachers, spin doctors, politicians, and other expert communicators.

Highlights
Books:

» (1988) *Influence, or how to work the system*. Century, London.

» (1992) *Personal Impact: The art of good communication*. Reed, London.

» (1998) *The Primacy Effect: The ultimate guide to personal communications skills*. Orion Business, London.

LEADERS ON COMMUNICATION

The quotes below are from a variety of leaders – business, political, spiritual, cultural, and military – giving their views on aspects of the communication process. They are included, without comment, as points to think about as you reflect on your communication skills and their effectiveness.

"You have not forgotten the important communication to Nemours? Good little woman."

Prince Albert's last words to Queen Victoria

"It's in the papers, it must be true."

Richard Branson, Chairman, Virgin Group

"Pictures are for entertainment, messages should be delivered by Western Union."

Sam Goldwyn

"If a playwright is funny, the English look for the serious message, and if he is serious they look for the joke."

Sacha Guitry

"In some modern literature there has appeared a tendency to replace communication by a private maundering to oneself which shall inspire one's audience to maunder privately to themselves – rather as if the author handed round a box of drugged cigarettes."

F.L. Lucas

"The medium is the message."

"Gutenberg made everybody a reader. Xerox makes everybody a publisher."

Marshall McLuhan

"So I started to use my junior high school English and the bits I knew of German and French, and I discovered I could communicate. Suddenly a group of travelers on a train found that everybody

had the same problems. We had English in common though, and although mine was rudimentary, it was good enough to be understood and it was accepted.''
Akio Morita, founder of Sony on why he wished his children to learn English

"Ability to listen to – and understand – what people are trying to communicate; and the ability to express oneself in a clear and concise way.''
Sadako Ogata, United Nations High Commissioner for Refugees (UNHCR) on the core values of UNHCR staff

"What Chekhov saw in our failure to communicate was something positive and precious: the private silence in which we live, and which enables us to endure our own solitude. We live, as his characters do, beyond any tale we happen to enact.''
V.S. Pritchett

"They never open their mouths without subtracting from the sum of human knowledge.''
Thomas Reed, late nineteenth-century Speaker of the House of Representatives, on members of Congress

"So business leaders have a choice: they can build a huge PR wall and talk down to customers or they can listen and respond.''
Anita Roddick

"We give people an opportunity to test, question, and disagree.''
Richard Semler, CEO, SEMCO

"I should but teach him how to tell my story.''
William Shakespeare, Othello

"Every picture tells a story.''
Sloan's Backache and Kidney Oils advertisement, 1907

"A short neck denotes a good mind. You see the messages go quicker to the brain because they've shorter to go.''
Muriel Spark

Communication
Resources

» General books book about communication.
» Subject-specific books.
» Magazines and journals useful when considering communication.
» Useful Websites.

RECOMMENDED READING

Bedeian, A. (1993) *Management*. Harcourt Brace, Orlando.

Black, J.S., Morrison, A.J. and Gregersen, H.B. (1999) *Global Explorers*. Routledge, New York.

Buzan, A. (1977) *Harnessing the Power of the Parabrain*. Colt, London.

Cartwright, R. (2001) *Managing Diversity*. Capstone, Oxford.

Cartwright, R. and Green, G. (1997) *In Charge of Customer Satisfaction*. Blackwell, Oxford.

Crainer, S. (1998) *Business the Rupert Murdoch Way*. Capstone, Oxford.

Davidson, M. and Bahl, K. (1997) *The Black and Ethnic Minority Woman Manager*. Paul Chapman, London.

Davidson, M. and Cooper, G. (1992) *Shattering the Glass Ceiling*. Paul Chapman, London.

Davies, C. (1997) *Divided by a Common Language*. Mayflower Press, Sarasota (FL).

Harris, P.R. and Moran, R.T. (2000) *Managing Cultural Differences*. Gulf Publishing Co., Houston.

Hastings, M. and Jenkins, S. (1983) *The Battle for the Falklands*. Michael Joseph, London.

Johnson, G. and Scholes, K. (1984) *Exploring Corporate Strategy*. Prentice Hall, Hemel Hempstead.

Klein, N. (2000) *No Logo: no space, no choice, no jobs, taking aim at the brand bullies*. Flamingo, London.

Korten, D. (1995) *When Corporations Rule the World*. Earthscan, London.

Lewis, R.D. (1999) *Cross-Cultural Communication: A visual approach*. Transcreen, London.

Lewis, R.D. (2000) *When Cultures Collide*. Nicholas Brealey, London.

Lorenz, K. (1966) *On Aggression*. Methuen, London.

Morris D, (1969) *The Human Zoo*. Jonathan Cape, London.

Nicholson, M. (2000) *Managing the Human Animal*. Crown, New York.

Ransom, D. (2001) *The No-Nonsense Guide to Fair Trade*. New Internationalist, Oxford.

Rolt, L.T.C. (1986) *Red for Danger*, 4th ed. Pan, London.

Shea, M. (1988) *Influence, or how to work the system*. Century, London.

Shea, M. (1993) *Personal Impact: The art of good communication*. Reed, London.

Shea, M. (1998) *The Primacy Effect: The ultimate guide to personal communications skills*. Orion Business, London.

Stith, A. (1996) *Breaking the Glass Ceiling: Racism and sexism in corporate America*. Bryant & Dillon, Orange (NJ).

Stith, A. (1999) *How to Build a Career in the New Economy: A guide for minorities and women*. Warwick Publishing, New York.

Trompenaars, F. (1993) *Riding the Waves of Culture*. Economist Books, London.

Wirth, L. (2000) *Breaking through the Glass Ceiling*. International Labor Organization, Geneva.

For information about communication in general

Cairncross, F. (1997) *The Death of Distance: How the communications revolution will change our lives*. Orion Business, London.

Cairncross, F. (2001) *The Death of Distance 2.0: How the communications revolution will change our lives*. Texere, London.

Heath, R.L. and Bryant, J. (1992) *Human Communication: Theory and research*. Lawrence Erlbaum Associates, New York.

McQuail, D. (1969) *Towards a Sociology of Mass Communications*. Macmillan, London.

McQuail, D. (ed.) (1972) *Sociology of Mass Communications: Selected readings*. Penguin, Harmondsworth.

McQuail, D. (1984) *Communication*, 2nd ed. Longman, London.

McQuail, D. (1992) *Media Performance: Mass communication in the public interest*. Sage, London.

McQuail, D. (1994) *Mass Communication Theory: An introduction*, 3rd ed. Sage, London.

McQuail, D. and Windahl, S. (1993) *Communication Models for the Study of Mass Communications*, 2nd ed. Longman, London.

Radtke, J. (1998) *Strategic Communications for Nonprofit Organizations*. John Wiley, New York.

For Information about e-mail as a communication tool

Flynn, N. and Flynn, T. (2000) *Writing Effective E-mail*. Kogan Page, London.

Flynn, N. and Flynn, T. (2000) *The E-policy Handbook*. Amacom, New York.

For information about the Internet

Aldrich, D.F. (1999) *Mastering the Digital Marketplace*. John Wiley, New York.

For information about American Express and Ken Chenault

Authers, J. (Feb. 27, 1997) "American Express president breaches white stronghold." Online at www.worldafricanet.com/news/newsinformation/news5.html

Ballen, K. (March 2, 1997) "People to watch." *Fortune Magazine*, New York.

Business Week (Jan. 1, 1998) "The 25 top managers of the year." *Business Week*, New York.

Marquardt, M.J. and Berger, N.O. (2000) *Global Leaders for the 21st Century*. State University of New York Press, Albany.

Pierce, P. (July, 1997) "Blazing new paths in corporate America." *Ebony Magazine*, New York.

For information about The Body Shop

Roddick, A. (1991) *Body and Soul: Profits with principles*. Ebury Press, London.

Roddick, A. (2000) *Business as Unusual*. HarperCollins, London.

For Information about HDFC

Dayao, D.L.C (ed.) (2000) *Asian Business Wisdom*. John Wiley, Singapore.

Ten Steps to Making Communication Work

The ten steps for effective communications are as follows.

1 Know the audience.
2 Choose the right code.
3 Eliminate or make allowance for noise.
4 Tell a story.
5 Don't let technology obscure the message.
6 Keep records.
7 Don't surprise people if you don't have to.
8 Remember the body language.
9 Learn to act.
10 Seek feedback.

And finally: *build up a network of contacts*.

Every communication and every audience is different. The leader should ensure that they have thought carefully about the message, whom it is for, how it will be transmitted, and how they will know that it has been understood. The ten steps below are designed to help achieve this.

1. KNOW THE AUDIENCE

Every good communicator – whether they are a business leader, a politician, a singer, or a stand-up comedian – makes sure that they know who the audience are. In that way they can adapt their material to the audience. The most successful comedians are those who use the experiences of the audience as the basis for their comedy – hence their reliance on news items for comic material.

The importance of a communication is not that it is made but that it is understood. This means putting the needs of the audience before those of the communicator. It is worth remembering that the communicator (usually) knows what the message is – the skill is in putting that message across and different audiences may need different approaches.

2. CHOOSE THE RIGHT CODE

As described in Chapter 6, the code is not just words and pictures but the tone, emphasis, and supplementaries such as body language included in the communication. Choosing the right code is important as it ensures that the correct degree of importance will be attached by the audience. Humor may well have a part to play but a very serious message, for example one affecting people's job security, should not be approached with any levity. Equally sometimes lightening the mood by the use of a carefully chosen humorous comment can be useful. Effective leaders possess a sensitivity to events and are able to code their communications in a manner that reflects the likely mood of the audience.

It is also vital that those receiving a communication can actually decode it. They need to speak the same "language." This does not just mean speaking in the same national language but in the same language register (see Chapter 6), and avoiding jargon unless the communicator is sure that the audience knows and understands the terms being used.

It is also important that both leader and audience recognize a similar meaning. The differences between American and British English are not immense but some terms can mean something completely different in the US than in the UK.

3. ELIMINATE OR MAKE ALLOWANCE FOR NOISE

It is probably impossible to eliminate all noise (as defined in Chapter 6), but much of the noise can be anticipated and allowed for, even if it cannot be totally eliminated. Ensuring that the message has been carefully thought out, and that there are no contradictions or ambiguous statements, is important. Making sure that the transmission is not interrupted in any way and that there is always a summary can also help reduce noise. Telling them what you are going to tell them, telling it to them, and then telling them what you have told them (see Chapter 6) also helps reduce the problems of misunderstanding through noise, as the key parts of the message will have been reinforced.

4. TELL A STORY

One of the early communication skills a child learns is to listen to a story. The effective leader can use the techniques and structure of storytelling to make the message as interesting as possible. Using stories from the relevant culture can assist in contextualizing the message, thus aiding understanding. This is a very ancient method of putting across complex ideas and philosophies.

5. DON'T LET TECHNOLOGY OBSCURE THE MESSAGE

You have probably been a member of an audience at a presentation where the person delivering it has used nearly every piece of communications and presentation technology they could lay their hands on. It is often very distracting, as the audience spends more time wondering "How did they do that?" than considering the core message of the presentation.

Technology exists to aid communication, not to hinder it. An inappropriate method of communication can mean that the message is distorted. As more and more means of communication become available, the leader needs to make sure that they neither offend people nor trivialize the message by selecting the wrong medium for transmitting it.

6. KEEP RECORDS

"I don't remember you saying that!" How often are these words heard in organizations (and homes) throughout the world! Without a record of communications, one can be left open to the charge that the communication was never made. E-mail and modern telephone equipment are useful in that they provide logs, the former also allowing for a copy to be preserved.

It is important to keep records of communications for future reference so that there is an audit trail. This does not mean that vast quantities of paper need to be kept, just brief notes. The writer has found it useful to keep a telephone log next to the telephone to record who telephoned (or was telephoned), the date and time of the call, what the subject was, and any action points. There is nothing worse than somebody saying "Remember when we spoke on the phone last week and you agreed to ... ?" It is difficult to respond if you cannot remember the conversation. A brief log can save a great deal of embarrassment. In more and more cases, courts are requiring logs and diaries to be produced as evidence of actions. Modern technology also allows for telephone conversations to be recorded, but in many jurisdictions it is illegal to do this without first informing the other party. It is also, of course, extremely bad manners.

7. DON'T SURPRISE PEOPLE IF YOU DON'T HAVE TO

Not everybody needs to receive a communication at the same time. It may be necessary to brief some staff before others. It is a poor leader who exposes their subordinates to having to comment on something about which they should know, but have never been informed.

Communications should only come like a bolt out of the blue in an emergency or crisis. At other times people should have a chance to receive a briefing. A poor leader might ask somebody to comment off the cuff; a good leader will say "Can we talk about X in an hour, which will give you a chance to review the paperwork and consult others?'' Good leaders do not go around trying to catch people out by ambushing them. It is better practice to "catch people in" – that way communication can be more effective because all parties are briefed about the subject. Even in meetings, AOB (any other business) does not mean that anything can be raised. That is pointless, as people may not have the necessary information to hand. AOB is at the end of an agenda to allow for discussion of anything that is on the agenda but has not been covered fully.

A good leader does not point to a document in their hand and ask for an explanation, unless they have informed the other person that they intend to raise the matter, thus allowing the other person to bring their copy with them. It may be part of a power game to place somebody at a disadvantage, but it shows poor communication skills and equally poor leadership.

8. REMEMBER THE BODY LANGUAGE

In any face-to-face communication, body language will convey a large part of the message. This includes the way you are dressed, the way you stand, your articulation, etc. If these are at variance with the message, the brain of a recipient will solve the dissonance created instinctively – it will be the body language message that is the one that will be accepted rather than the one intended.

Leaders ignore body language at their peril and need to remember that when they are gesticulating at the end of the telephone, their agitation may be perceived through their tone of voice even though they cannot be seen. Whilst this may seem self-evident, body language is so instinctive that we continue to use it even when we know we cannot be seen. Just watch your colleagues when they are having telephone conversations – are they animated?

Body language can be hard to control but it is not impossible to do so – see step 9 below.

9. LEARN TO ACT

The communication skills of a good leader are similar to those of a successful actor or actress. They are able to put themselves into a part and because they are aware of the totality of the message – words, tone, body language, etc. – they are able to "fool" an audience into believing that they are somebody else.

It is not the suggestion that leaders should be fooling people all the time, but there may be times when their true feelings are not to be shown. A few years ago the writer of this material went to watch a friend perform. The friend is a successful singer and recording artist. The performance was superb. What the audience did not know and would not have guessed was that it was the first public performance since the death of his son in a tragic accident. A performer knows that, as the old saying goes, "the show must go on." A good leader will be able to exude confidence when communicating, even if that is not what they feel or they are having domestic problems. People need confidence in their leaders, a point made by Desmond Morris (see Chapter 3). Accordingly, the leader may have to act a part for the good of the organization. This takes practice and control but is a necessary part of the leader's communication skills.

10. SEEK FEEDBACK

Communication without feedback is next to useless. It is feedback that shows whether a message has been understood. Many accidents and tragedies would have been prevented if those issuing instructions had checked whether the recipient's understanding was the same as theirs. Just asking "Did you understand that?" is totally useless. What is required is a knowledge of what was understood. Many people will answer "Yes" because they believe that they have understood.

Acting sensitively, a good leader will ask questions to ensure that all parties have an equal understanding. If there are differences, either the leader has not communicated properly or there is a training need for those who have somehow got the wrong end of the stick.

And finally there is a most important 11th step that every good communicator must take and that is to *build up your network* as described in Chapter 6.

KEY LEARNING POINTS

» There are steps that leaders and potential leaders can take to ensure effective communication.
» To communicate effectively, the leader has to combine skills related to storytelling, technology, acting and body language.
» Communication without feedback is not proper communication.

Frequently Asked Questions (FAQs)

Q1: What are the components of a communication system?

A: To be communicated effectively, a message must be *coded* into a format all parties understand, *transmitted* by a suitable means, and *decoded* by the recipient. Then *feedback* must be sought to ensure that the understanding is shared by the sender and recipient. There is more on this process in Chapter 6.

Q2: What is meant by the term noise?

A: Noise is anything that interferes with, or distorts, the communication process. It does not have to be physical. Jargon, misconceptions, coding errors, and decoding errors are all examples of noise, as explained in Chapter 6.

Q3: How can the Internet help with communication?

A: Computers, the Internet, e-mail, and videoconferencing have greatly speeded up the communication process, making distance less of a barrier to effective communication. They are not, however, ideal for transmitting feelings and emotions, and should not be used for this purpose unless absolutely necessary. The use of technology, especially the Internet, for communication purposes is covered in Chapter 4.

Q4: How important is a cultural understanding of the recipient?

A: Very important. Different cultures have differing norms about how communication should be carried out. Some cultures are very formal regarding business communication, whilst others are not. In some cultures it is permissible to get straight to the point, whereas in others social intercourse should precede business matters. As organizations become more global in nature, these cultural issues are becoming more and more important. You can read more about this question in Chapter 5.

Q5: Should one always seek feedback?

A: Without proper feedback it is impossible to be sure that there is mutual understanding. Just asking whether something has been understood is not feedback. Feedback involves checking that a person actually knows what they are expected to do, etc. Feedback should always be sought. There is a discussion on feedback in Chapter 6.

Q6: Is communication a learnt skill or an inherent one?

A: As primates, human beings come preprogrammed with a set of inherent communication skills, which are built on during childhood. Presentation and linguistic skills, however, have to be learnt and cultural sensitizing is often necessary. Once one becomes aware of inherent factors such as body language, it becomes easier to exert a measure of conscious control. Even inherent skills can be improved upon by study and practice. You can read more about this in Chapter 3.

Q7: How important is a knowledge of body language?

A: Body language is the subconscious way most of us indicate our true feelings. Actors and actresses are able to suppress their natural body language and use that of the character. It is hard to suppress body language, as it is designed to provide signals to others of the same species. If one is defensive, worried, or confident, this shows through in the poses one adopts. Knowing about it gives the individual more control over their body language and helps ensure that the message of the words matches the message of the body language. There is more about body language in Chapters 3 and 6.

Q8: Is it necessary for a leader to possess foreign language skills in order to be a good communicator?

A: Obviously it helps if the leader can speak other languages but, if this is not possible, even a minimal ability to use salutations and to say please and thank you in the tongue of a recipient can go a long way towards breaking the ice. The more the leader can put somebody at their ease, the smoother the communication process is likely to be. Language difficulties can constitute a great deal of noise, as defined above. This is covered in Chapters 5 and 6.

Q9: Why are communications always referred to as a minimum of two-way?

A: Whilst it might seem obvious that there must be at least two parties in a communication (even when talking to oneself, it is different aspects of the personality that are in conversation), without feedback a communication is not really that at all – it may be meaningless words. The two-way concept denotes that communication is not a linear process but a loop. There is more about this in Chapter 6.

Q10: Where are resources available to assist in understanding the communication aspects of leadership?

A: A list of books, journals, and Web addresses will be found in Chapter 9.

Index

9 781841 123646

9 781841 123646